A Curious Tradition

Marriage Among Christians

A Curious Tradition

Marriage Among Christians

James Tunstead Burtchaell, c.s.c.

and Eugene S. Geissler
Sally Cunneen
Robert Engler
Dorothea Cordova Engler
Richard Conklin
Rosemary Haughton
Margery Frisbie
Thomas Shaffer
Photography by
Stephen Moriarty

Ave Maria Press·Notre Dame, Indiana 46556

Acknowledgments:

For excerpts from *Tell Me a Riddle* by Tillie Olsen. Copyright ©
1956, 1957, 1960, 1961 by Tillie Olsen. Reprinted by permission
of Delacorte Press/Seymour Lawrence.

For excerpts from *Yonnondio From the Thirties* by Tillie Olsen.
Copyright © 1974 by Tillie Olsen. Reprinted by permission of
Delacorte Press/Seymour Lawrence.

Library of Congress Catalog Card Number: 77-81396
International Standard Book Number: 0-87793-139-9

Cover photograph by Eugene J. Zehring, Sr.
Inside photographs by Stephen Moriarty

Manufactured in the United States of America

Dedicated
to
All the Families
in My Wedding Album

Contents

An Introduction

This is a book about the facts of life. Nobody ever seems to be told the facts of life by his or her parents. I suppose most parents could bring themselves to tell their youngsters the physical facts of sex. They find it immensely more difficult to tell their sons and daughters the intimacies of their personal life together, and this is what the facts of life are really all about. Occasionally, in a very sad moment of distress, or in the glow of much wine, a parent will be eased into this sort of sharing with a child, but not often as easily as the same parent might open up to someone else's child who grew up next door or lived down the street.

Traditionally, other people than their parents have told young folk about marriage. When I was a college student, about 25 years ago, a book came out which was supposed to offer the last word on marriage. It was coauthored by a priest and a doctor. The only trouble was that the priest's part presented the Holy Family of Nazareth as an ideal for marriage and the doctor's part was a plumbing manual about sex. Somehow one stumbled at imagining that a household with a mother pregnant out of wedlock, parents who had no sex, and a son who, like an only child, spent his childhood delivering precocious one-liners, was a family that had much to offer by way of example. Nor was the reader likely to know what sex was all about just by having the *corpus luteum* explained.

In a milder manner this same problem sometimes beset the conferences our Church has been accustomed to offer engaged couples for the last decades. Often a priest and a doctor and a social worker would make presentations that were professionally on the mark, but somehow didn't always blend into a single coherent and attractive picture. In time, more helpful talks were given by married couples who had little professional involvement in other people's homes, but spoke candidly and attractively about their own. Nowadays, successful premarital presentations seem to take place in the homes of couples who invite groups of engaged people to spend evenings with them and share experiences and thoughts on marriage.

This book is written by a number of people who are married (except for the the editor who, using the Alfred M. Hitchcock privilege, has slipped in among his invited performers). I do not know that we are all that wise. Wisdom comes from experience, and the friends who, so to speak, are inviting our readers into their living rooms reach into their own experiences and also into those of other folk beside and behind them. From what others learned yesterday we have learned to squint at today's experiences, and they have told us more this way than otherwise. This is what a tradition does. We think that this learning has been going on at the Lord's prompting, goaded and teased and tutored by his help. This is what revelation is and does. Though in the end it does not make any of us all that wise, we want to pass on the sourdough to others for them to use as a starter, grateful that it was saved for us to use, and hopeful that even better bakers will come along to use the old yeast.

For an institution so widely practiced, Christian marriage (and indeed any variety of marriage) seems to have produced a very scarce number of helpfully articulate practitioners. It is a tradition that has gone under the cloud of contempt lately, and has also been enfogged by a lot of uncertainty and debate in just the past few years. But there is a tradition there, and my own propensity is to think more of it each day. Yet it has so few spokesmen — at least spokesmen that one does not find embarrassing. The tradition is as follows.

Jesus surprised his followers by inviting them to a novel kind of marital commitment: for better or for worse, until death. It was an unremitting promise of fidelity, free of conditions on which one could and might withdraw, and it was the ground for both a more demanding love and a more secure trust. His followers found it a crazy sort of commitment, and he admitted it was, but said the Father made it possible, just as he empowered men and women to quit their attachments to believe in and follow him.

This sort of commitment is desperately difficult to live up to, and older believers urge younger ones to approach these promises with care and caution. It being the decision of a lifetime, one has to plumb through the high feelings of affection to find a deeper, firmer ground to rest it on, and there is a wisdom about what are good grounds for marrying and what are unreliable ones. The first times together bring their surprises, and it is a demanding task to smelt two persons into one household. Ironically, one cannot count on marriage changing one's partner's insufficiencies, yet that is exactly what one hopes from marriage.

Sex is meant to embody that surrender of privacy which comes from belonging to each other. It celebrates what marriage is, and has been given a deeper sense and joy by Christians who make these deeper promises. It is not best understood simply as an expression of love; rather, it embodies belonging — belonging in a way that only marriage quite achieves. The love of marriage should have a welcome to sharers, particularly children. The planning of birth is a reasonable thing, but there should be in the hearts of husbands and wives enough hunger and reverence for children that family limitation would be accepted with some reluctance, and abortion not thought of.

The opportunities for women in society are being abruptly opened, and our tradition needs a severe jolt in its understanding of how families grow when both parents, or just the wife-mother, are active in careers. On this there is much learning to be done, but there are some cautionary things that can be shared with beginners on the road — to avoid anger and a sense that marriage is the stifler of freedom. Bad times are often good times in retrospect, and the humor, patience, tolerance and sobriety which should belong to more experienced spouse-parents can at least be mooted before the young. The growth of marriages goes on and on and on. The adventures continue, and so do the challenges. There are times to grow when your children grow, and when they leave you, and when they have their own children, and when you are widowed. These experiences seem so far off to those approaching marriage, but should be at least glimpsed by them.

This congested and clotted précis is unworthy of the inherited cherishing of marriage we have commonly received. Unfortunately, there are so many young people who know not even this much of it. Somehow their parents either disbelieved it or never took it in, but I see young folk marrying helter-skelter without even a suspicion of this awesome vision. They marry for better, not for worse. They speak of love, but it is something that happens to them, not something they do. Children are a burden to be indefinitely postponed. They couple in the teeth of clashing disagreements over basic values, and count on some future blending to bind them together, rather than confronting or even discussing their values beforehand. They mate when they are not mates, and seem never to have had it put to them cogently that sex means what marriage means — or that it means anything at all. They anticipate a future of a year or so, not of a lifetime.

And so we wrote this book. It makes no attempt to tell anyone how to marry. But it tries to offer to those married, and to those who will marry, and to those who help the married, some ideas to think upon.

Let me say a word about the individual chapters. My own contribution expounds a view, peculiar to Christians, that marriage ought be more drastic, more outright in self-surrender. It argues, I suppose, that much of the "better" grows out of the "worse."

Gene Geissler has written some very powerful books about his large family. I asked him for a chapter on the successive adventures wherein the growth of children forces the growth of parents. Birth, childhood, adolescence, leaving, marrying, giving birth to grandchildren, losing some family, losing one's partner: all of these call out of a person things he or she had never intended.

I wanted Sally Cunneen to give us a chapter on the changes in marriage provoked by changes in the situation of women. How can they take up their new and rightful opportunities and still do justice to their children? How can men be reeducated to understand that their family is not a pit-crew for their careers, and that they are going to have to withdraw some of their aggressive energies from their work and redirect that power toward their homes?

The youngest writers are Bob and Dotty Engler, and they write about two-becoming-one and still being distinct individuals. They describe how easily one partner can submit to the other, rather than working toward the fuller human partnership of two in one flesh, mind, work, heart.

Dick Conklin works with me at a university, and for the interest of readers facing marriage I wished him to write about home-making and home-breaking without commitment. He speaks of the irony that what makes marriage so enduring is the large risk involved.

Rosemary Haughton has written an entirely different sort of chapter — no autobiography, though she is author, lecturer, and mother of 10 children. She shreds the prevailing romantic myth of love and marriage, suggesting in its stead a myth of heroism. It is a very serious essay.

To Margery Frisbie I wrote: "What I am asking you for is a chapter on fidelity when it is really put to the test. I need you to convince young folk, who look forward to joy, that there is a deep sense in being true to family when there is no pay-off in joy. In a sense this should be the toughest chapter in the book to write. You can, I think."

Tom Shaffer I asked to write on children as of the promises of marriage, as of the need of life. There is a presumption against children today, and since he has been good to his own and to others', he speaks of welcoming them rather than flinching.

We believe in what we write.

J.T.B.
Killarney Point
Land O'Lakes, Wisconsin
Lady Day in August, 1976

1. For Better, For Worse
James Tunstead Burtchaell, c.s.c.

James Tunstead Burtchaell, Notre Dame's theologian-provost, is a rarity among priest-educators in living in a campus residence hall. This is not a comfortable concession to the symbolism of community. It is, matter of fact, unwelcomed noise at night. It is counseling at hours seldom of one's choosing. It is patience in the face of pranks. It is vulnerability to human transactions when one wishes privacy. It is confronting others' problems when one longs for time to solve one's own.

But it is also rewarding comradeship, shared amidst the corrective of human commerce. It is teaching in the deepest sense of that important word. It is ethics in situ. *It is coaxing others into growing up . . . and realizing that one matures by doing so.*

James Burtchaell is graced with a pen the equal of his insight. He is especially talented at drawing out the persistent wisdom at the core of our religious tradition. He deftly takes that enduring deposit of "oughtness" (which causes people to establish churches in the first place), and tests it against the recurrent skepticism of reexperiencing believers, as well as against the honest — and pervasive — dissent of nonbelievers.

Marriage has not been a subject which the sacerdotal ministry of the Roman Catholic Church has been prepared to treat convincingly. It is all the more refreshing, then, to see Father Burtchaell remind us of distinctive characteristics of our marriages we know better . . . but have never said as well.

Richard Conklin

1. For Better, For Worse

There are many new formats for marriage being suggested and tried out in recent times. Some seem rather peculiar. One of the oddest sorts of marriage (though not very new) still continues to be the Christian usage customary among Catholics. I am going to try to show the sense underneath this Christian tradition. It is not exclusive to Catholics, nor are they always so single-mindedly faithful to it, but it is in that denomination that this Christian tradition has most tenaciously been honored.

At the outset one thing needs to be said clearly: there is no orthodox policy which recognizes only a single legitimate way for folk to marry — our way — and insists that other arrangements should somehow be suppressed. Quite the contrary: our particular custom of marriage is so strange that one could not expect it to make much sense to those not of our Christian household. Only within the context of a peculiar faith would such marriage not seem strange. Our matrimony promises just about the same things that our baptism does. People who think that this bunch of Christians is generally sensible and sober about its religion but a little peculiar in its views on matrimony are really quite wrong. We are crazy in every way.

If in a certain society a man is permitted to have six wives, then the Church has neither warrant nor wish to tell him that he only *thinks* he has six, whereas in reality one is the limit and five must go. If a man desires to acquire spouses by the half-dozen, the State may say him nay; but if the State allows it then our Church must simply acknowledge that he has six helpmates, legitimate yet possibly problematic (though it be our private thought that, in the matter of spouses, less is more). If in a certain culture it is accepted that men and women marry only for as long as they wish and can then be free to remarry others — well, we refrain from muttering that this is only licensed concubinage. If people set out to marry, then they are married. Marriage is what one makes it — or what two make it. Societies have developed some quite diverse ways of doing it. We can consider our way more promising without claiming that all other ways are illegitimate.

One hears the complaint that the Church is at its most legalistic on issues of marriage and divorce, and that it ought to reform its legislation in the way that most countries have. But it is the State, not the Church, which asserts its right to govern the processes of marriage and divorce by law. The State insists on its right to license (and in some countries to witness) marriages, and to grant divorces on its terms. By contrast with the State, and with what many imagine, the Church has no comparable corpus of law controlling marriage and forbidding divorce. Such regulations as exist bind the churchmen themselves more than those who propose to marry or unmarry. Admittedly there is a lot of activity in our chanceries and curia that gives off the sound and smell of legalism. Some of it has no excuse as, for example, when the Church tries to bully a country into recognizing only the Catholic usage of marriage (previously the case in Italy, no better than the present laws in Israel which oblige all Jews to observe Orthodox Jewish usages). No Christian church should claim any more than the right all citizens have to use the political process to press for marriage laws which seem best to them. Still, what passes for legalistic business in Church precincts does not involve clergy telling laity how and where and if they may marry. It involves, rather, churchmen determining for themselves when they may celebrate marriages truthfully and in adequate consistency with both faith and good sense. As a priest, I cannot with full conscience and exuberance officiate at a marriage which seems to be folly from the start. If I decline to do so, I am not telling a couple they cannot marry; I am saying that I cannot see my way clear to leading them in this celebration. Actually, rather than being less finicky about who is married, we might well become more so about who is baptized and who ordained.

The point is that the Church does not control or govern marriage. Its mission is to celebrate, rather than to legislate. It *preaches* marriage: a particular sort of marriage in a particular sort of spirit. It celebrates marriage, though only its own kind. It encourages people to give their whole hearts to one another in marriage. It rallies support for those who have undertaken to do so, and it grieves for those who suffer in or abandon their marriages. But unlike the State it does not and cannot constrain people to practice what it preaches.

Surely, one objects, the Church has laws forbidding divorce. No, it does not. The Church since Paul has insisted that there is one bond with higher claims than marriage: the bond of faith. If the two bonds come atangle, it is the bond of marriage which can be undone to unsnarl the bond of faith. But when confronted with a marriage that is in and of the faith, the Church has no laws on divorce. Quite the contrary: it confesses its incompetence to devise any law that could presume to dissolve oaths made to be indissoluble. It claims to lack authority to declare its marriages finished and to celebrate new ones atop the ruins of the old. This is not so much for want of warrant from Jesus or from the scriptures, nor even out of stubborn insistence on its own ancient tradition, but because no one has ever sensibly explained how these promises, freely and knowingly made, "for better, for worse, until death," could truthfully and meaningfully be made to another person before death, no matter how bad the "worse" had become. The Church believes it can invite its members to enter some undertakings which are beyond its own power to govern.

Part of today's confusion regarding matrimony comes from the fact that so many wedding rituals deceive. Unfortunately, most civil jurisdictions in the Western world, and also most Christian denominations, use marriage rituals that are descended and adapted from the old Catholic rites. Not adapted enough, perhaps. Men and women, through one formulary or another, are led by judges and ministers into promises they may not really mean. They are being made to say that they bind themselves solemnly by oath to one another for life. Yet neither the State nor their Church nor their society nor the couple themselves has any such understanding of what is being promised. What is really meant is that a man and woman will remain faithfully as husband and wife as long as it pleases them to do so, and that they *expect,* but do not *pledge,* that their union will last until death. The promises should be reshaped according to what people mean, and people might then be less deceived. In fact, most marriage rituals should probably omit all talk of promise, pledge, or oath. So many couples do not *do* something at their wedding; they announce that something *has happened* to them. They regard their marriage as a public declaration of a joyful compatibility they hope will endure; they do not give themselves to one another irrevocably in such a way as to expect that there will be seasons when both joy and compatibility seem lost in the fog and clouds, and promise that even then they will sail on.

If the State and the many Churches rewrote their marriage rituals to conform to what they really expect of brides and grooms, two things would follow. There would be considerably less disjunction between the ungrounded romanticism at the time of marriage and the unrelieved defeatism at the time of divorce. And we should see fewer counterculture experiments in trial marriages, prenuptial property agreements, contract cohabitation, etc., when it is clearly understood that these are merely legitimate variants on the kind of marriage our society generally promotes, and not really so distinct from it.

Let every tradition, every society, every Church and every State — even every man and woman — make such marriages as they please. The Christians I speak of ask only the freedom to offer their children a kind of promising that is more promising, a kind of undertaking that is more dreadful, a kind of joy that is more firmly grounded. We do not claim to prevent failure, either by assuring spouses that they will inevitably live up to their promises or by reducing the substance of the promises to the point where virtually nothing is committed and so any forfeiture is not very great. The Church does, however, claim that failure, even the most miserable, can be swallowed up in forgiveness. It even hints that there are some kinds of success — these the most exquisite — which seem to grow only in the soil of failure. The Church has no right to despise other traditions and ventures, even though it notices that many accommodations made to human failure are only too likely to invite and then compound that ever-present failure.

Having said all this, I must acknowledge what every reader has already noticed: that this vision of marriage, while native to the mind of the Church, is not at home in the mind of every communicant. It has taken mean and misshapen forms at times, and has assumed a shrill harshness foreign to Jesus' message, to which we owe a better and more faithful presentation.

It would be senseless for our Christian band to hold out our vision of marriage to those who do not share our vision of Jesus and the faith. Still worse to press it upon them. Better for us to understand both visions ourselves, and live both better — and then to explain how we see faith in the Father of Jesus and fidelity to a sworn spouse as similarly promised, and successful on similar strengths, and undertaken with similarly crazy risks.

*   *   *

It has been believed by Catholics that, on a cue from Jesus, Christians developed a remarkable new way of marrying. Scattered through the Gospels are traces of the two basic sayings of Jesus on the subject: "What God has united, man must not divide" (Mk 10:9; Mt 19:6); and "The man who divorces his wife and marries another is guilty of adultery against her" (Mk 10:11; Mt 19:9; Lk 16:18).

The sense of Jesus' teaching shows clearest in the context given it by Matthew in his 19th chapter. The chapter presents two scenarios, told in a fashion parallel to each other. In the latter of the two stories Jesus is approached by a young man who obviously intends to draw out the traveling rabbi and probe his program and emphasis. He asks a standard leading question: "Master, what good deed must I do to possess eternal life?" Jesus' answer is, to start with, a standard one. He cites some of the more familiar commandments about not giving perjured evidence, not killing, not committing adultery, and the like. The young man warms to this teaching, for he claims to have kept these commandments since childhood. Is there anything else to be done? Indeed there is. Jesus goes on to say that if he wishes to complete the task he must sell all his possessions, give the proceeds to the poor, and join Jesus in his wanderings. At this the young man's smile fades and, instead of joining Jesus' retinue, he disappears in the opposite direction. The writer tells us that he would have had a large estate to liquidate.

The disciples, who had not had long to contemplate the prospect of having a rich man (even a formerly rich man) in their group, seem to have wondered 'whether a more discreet response by Jesus might have kept the young recruit from being frightened away. But Jesus takes them aside and makes his meaning even stiffer: it would be easier to thread a needle with a camel than for a rich man to possess eternal life. There is no mistaking his message now, and in dismay they comment that this is mad: on these terms no one would ever make the attempt. Yes, says Jesus: now they begin to glimpse the point. It is indeed crazy, but God can and will give folk the strength to do it. Then, lest they imagine that he is speaking simply of wealth, he tells them that a man must leave behind kin, property and land to rove about with him. They must, in a word, quit home with its security and its providing and its reciprocation of support, and go wandering about after him among the world's strangers, on the prowl for those in need.

Jesus, in Matthew's Gospel, repeatedly repudiates the religion of his time and place in ways that would have applied as well to religions of other times, places and peoples. He directs his criticism toward what the Jews treasured as a most valuable benefit from God: the Law. A Jew felt that Law was a relief, not a burden. Unlike other peoples, the Jews had been told — and in some detail — what it was God expected of them. To come before the living God one day was dreadful enough; far worse and more terrifying to do so without a hint of what terms one would be judged on. The more explicit the Law, then, the better the boon.

This was a gift to be taken up zestfully. When a young man entered into his years of adult responsibility he accepted his divinely specified obligations. He entered life with open eyes; he knew what he was undertaking. This undertaking, however, was disdained by Jesus as insufficient. The Father's claims were limitless, as was his love. No laws could quite contain them. From men and women he required an endless service, an open-ended dedication. At no point could one say that one had satisfied God's claims on him; at the end everyone would have to wring his hands and admit that he was an unprofitable servant. No, God's claims were measured, not by a specified set of commandments or duties, but by the limitless misery and need of all fellow humans and by the limitless love wherewith Jesus had addressed himself to this want. Jesus called on his followers to move beyond a religion of laws and to take on one of dedication to persons and their service. This did not mean that behavior forbidden under the old laws now became acceptable. On the contrary, the new commandment summoned from mankind ever so much more tough a program of compliance. It was far more unsettling, since one could never know in advance just what his service would have to be, or how much would be required of him. By choosing to follow Jesus in his least brethren one was walking into the unknown. There would be many who, like the young man, preferred to do it by commandments, rather than put their whole heart and strength into his service. Their reach, sadly, would not extend quite far enough to put eternal life within their grasp.

Now the other story in Matthew 19 is a twin of that one. Jesus is approached by a group of devout religionists who want to know where he stands in a contemporary religious controversy. Some rabbis had held that adultery was the only legitimate ground for divorce; others were allowing that lesser grievances would justify it. Where did Jesus stand: with the conservatives or with the liberals?

With neither. He stormed at them that divorce for any reason was evil in God's sight, and had only been a concession by Moses to the mean spirits of the people. (Do not be misled by his exception, "except for unchastity," which Matthew added to Jesus' original saying to account for consanguineous Gentile convert couples, obliged to separate by the predominantly Jewish Christian Church which regarded such unions as incestuous and "unchaste.") Here, too, Jesus' disciples, as startled as his questioners, draw him aside and suggest that he had possibly overstated his point, that he really must have meant to be more tactful and moderate than he sounded. Not at all. Jesus restates himself even more trenchantly. If a man is cuckolded and abandoned, and as a result suffers the worst imaginable misfortune — being left childless, no better than a eunuch — even then he should stand fast and faithful and be reckoned happy in the kingdom. (At this point, lest his readers think that Jesus is down on children, Matthew introduces the playground scene where Jesus welcomes the youngsters ignored by the disciples.) This is crazy, his disciples warn, and impossible besides. Few would risk a marriage that

allowed of no escape. Insane, yes; impossible, no, rejoins
Jesus. It is, again, one of those crazy things God can make
the human heart capable of.

When a young Jew married, the limits of his undertaking
were known in advance. The acceptable grounds for divorce,
after all, served to describe and delimit the contours of his
commitment. He entered with open eyes. He knew what his
obligations would be, for they were revealed to him from the
start. But Jesus, in repudiating divorce, is commending a
radically different sort of marriage. One would bind oneself
to a person, rather than to a specific set of conditions or duties.
One's duties would be measured, not by a code subscribed to
and calculated in advance, but by another person's needs,
needs which can never quite be calculated beforehand, and
seem never conclusively to be served to the limit. Jesus calls
men and women to a union that is more frightening because
the legitimate claims on one's generosity are open-ended.

The unlimited baptismal surrender to the Lord in his
brethren is copied and embodied and specified in the surrender of matrimony. Both religion and marriage are transformed, and both similarly: each had been determined by
law; now each would be determined by human need and by
divine generosity. Each had required obedience. Now that
would not go far enough, and love — love without limits —
would be the better grounding virtue. Put another way:
obedience was not being retired from service; it was being
laid under obligation to new commands revealed in the un-
written law of one's neighbor's need. Some participants would
be called to render astonishingly sacrificial service, far beyond
their imagining or their strength. Both commitments — baptism and marriage — would summon forth fathomless faith,
if one were to have enough trust to follow another pledge-
person — spouse or Lord — wherever that might lead.

A marriage that can be dissolved is a marriage of hedged
love, just as a religion that can be satisfied by obedience to a
set law is a religion of hedged love. Jesus invites men and
women to pledge unhedging, reckless promises to one another.

And so, not knowing what lies before them, they promise to
be true to one another, for better, for worse, for richer, for
poorer, in sickness and in health, until death. Crazy. But no
more so than the other oath to love the Lord with their whole
heart and soul and strength, and to love one another as he
has loved them.

The stupendous difference of these promises does not
emerge as a gutsy determination to survive the crises that rise
up amid anyone's married life. It shows itself at the very
threshold of life together. It affects the promises made at
marriage time, and the temper of their keeping from that day.
A man and woman pledge themselves, not to joy or to peace
or to satisfaction, but to fidelity, from which joy and peace
and satisfaction are believed to spring. They do not proclaim
their delight and then hope that it will carry them through
duty. They vouch for duty and accept what delight that will
bring. The bond is so different from every other marriage
bond — from the outset.

*   *   *

At this point something should be said about pledging.
It is the ancient observation of nearly everyone that humans
arrive in life caring about themselves, and that they are un-
cannily disposed to remain that way. It is the ancient belief
of Christians that with God's help — and others', too — we
can grow forth from this self-centeredness into love — and
that we urgently need to do so. One of the most potent
strategies for emerging from egotism into love is pledging.
To pledge is to put oneself at another's service, to give someone a *claim* upon oneself.

Pledge yourself to another and you are doubly constrained. You are now obliged to be of service, no matter
how you or your circumstances or your pledge-person should
change. Secondly, the measure of your giving must be, not
your own preference, but the other person's needs. It is no
longer a matter of doing good for someone. One gives to
others a claim upon oneself and the immensity and urgency
of that claim, depending upon the developing needs of others,

lie beyond one's control. There come surprises, disappointments, and sacrifices; ironically one can know they are bound to come, yet when they arrive they have strange names and unfamiliar faces. A pledged person, in short, is repeatedly summoned to greater cherishing than he or she had planned, or perhaps wished.

Pledging appears to be a yielding up of choice, a mortgaging of say-so over one's own affairs. More shrewdly seen, it is really a constraint that renders life more voluntary. Precisely by rising to meet one's commitments a person grows to have a greater and more giving will. There is always the fear that, pledges once made, one will see the other person change. The affection and trust may then dissolve, leaving one bound to carry out commitments joylessly or alone. Those who are held back by this fear imagine that it is attraction to another which supports fidelity and makes it agreeable. The contrary is more often true. It is in keeping our pledges to people that we both notice and invite them to be even more attractive than we had first seen or they had first been. Affection is a weak and fickle foundation for service. Service, though, is the best ground affection is ever likely to have.

Christian marriage is as awesome a pledge as one human being can give to another: for better, for worse, until death. In fact, its only adequate model is the faith we pledge to the Lord or, better still, the faith he pledges to us. In both cases we attempt to respond to and reproduce in ourselves the fidelity pledged to us by God who is Fidelity himself. Between man and wife it is as between disciple and Jesus: one will be loved, one can claim to be loved, whatever one's faults. One need not be anxious whether one will continue to be cherished. One is literally forgiven before the fall.

We need not imagine that making pledges guarantees we shall keep them. Sacrifice of our convenience to another's need, after all, rubs against the grain. But we have to remember that the strength to make good on these promises is itself promised. And whoever lives faithfully and generously in marriage need never fear forfeiture on larger claims. There are none larger.

Perhaps this is why thoughtful Catholics are not dissuaded from their curious tradition by the obvious warning that one who leaves oneself so entirely at the mercy of another takes a mighty risk and may be steering into bitter sorrow. It is an even more basic article of faith that all Christian sacramental pledges are taken facing Jesus crucified, that no pledge can lead us around suffering, and that no pledge is great if it does not somehow pass us through fire and sorrow. Pledged marriage is a little like childbirth. Afterwards everyone tells you how marvelous it was, but it took a lot of pain and struggle to get to that point.

The Christian tradition shows itself skeptical about a person's ability to come to full human maturity or to possess eternal life without pledging oneself to some other people: for better, for worse, until death. The young man in Matthew's story had the disadvantage of being rich, the sort of fellow who was likely to lay claims easily on others, while evading theirs on him. Wealth, though, is only one of many claim-evaders. We are stubbornly selfish creatures. We are not likely to grow unless committed. To pledge without recourse is to expose ourselves to risk — but not to any risk that was not already there. For what it takes to serve our bondsmen when they are ill-tempered and ungrateful and mean and infuriating is nothing more than what we must in any case possess if we are to grow up. It is difficult to serve anyone; more difficult to do so when the terms of service are unspecified; and most difficult when there is no end to the service. Only one thing in the world is more difficult: to serve only those one likes, to the extent that it is agreeable, and for as long as one pleases. This is not just difficult; it is impossible. For on these unpledged terms we end up serving no one but ourselves. That is why we must pledge.

*   *   *

If what you accomplish in Christian marriage is to be bound for life, for better or for worse, then courtship is one of life's supremely important seasons. You are faced with the most important of choices, and the wisdom or the folly of the choice will cling to your soul for life — indeed, one could say that it is one of those decisions whose outcome reaches beyond death.

The crisis, however, is not so much to choose the right person as to choose how to marry the person of your choice. I have often had the impression, when homes and hearts are broken by divorce, that the cause of hostility and separation was not an unsuitability of the parties for each other. In fact, it is very difficult to discover basic marital "incompatibilities" which are beyond anyone's control; they tend to be very basic human faults that no one wishes to control. The cause of failure seemed to be that the couple had not really given themselves away to each other. If this hunch is correct, then whom one marries is less important than how. Yet one of the best ways to find out the kind of marriage you are headed for is to look at the kind of person you wish to marry and try to understand what draws you together.

Let me try to use a few commonplace examples to illustrate. Boy marries girl because of her slim figure, and only later discovers that her wits are similarly slender. Girl has been too long stifled at home, and will marry anyone who wants to emancipate her. Boy marries pregnant girl (who decided to get pregnant) because then she and their parents will no longer hold him guilty. Girl marries boy who has apparently walked away from a tragic marriage in which he was misunderstood and misappreciated. (I would apologize for these melodramatic examples if they happened less often.) What is the disaster? In these circumstances it is very easy to marry the wrong person. It is extremely difficult, in fact, to marry a right person. This rarely means, however, that a decent person falls foolish victim to a rotten one. People most often get what they deserve in marriage. Most anyone who marries the wrong person is himself or herself also the wrong person. More to the point: the marriage is wrong, often wrong from the start, and made wrong by two persons who, whatever their faults, might have married well — even to the same partners.

Is the bond between a couple generous or selfish? Granted that in the most good-hearted courtships there is and should be a pleasure and a passion and much merrymaking, the soundness of any prospective marriage has to be estimated by how prepared the man and woman are to sacrifice their own preferences for each other without brooding over it. This is a difficult judgment to make, and most difficult for those who have the most at stake. The most critical judgment of a lifetime has to be made before enough lifetime has passed by to make one very critical in judging. The most frivolous courtships and the most wonderful courtships generally feel the same to their chief participants. How are the parties facing engagement to form a reasonable and trustable judgment about themselves?

No one seems to ask parents anymore. I suspect it is not so much the young who don't want to ask as their elders who don't quite know how to answer. Once upon a time our society required folks to stay married, and parents told their children whom to marry. Time passed, and there followed a period when society still expected you to stay married, but you were left free to choose your own spouse. Today, after further change, society leaves you free to decide whom to marry, and similarly free to keep your promises or not. This, we are told, is social progress. In the literature of that middle period (I think particularly of turn-of-the-century novels that still portrayed young men asking old men for permission to marry their daughters, or at least their approval) the ideal parents were shown as those who were wise enough not to impose their own judgment on the youngsters. Today, though, I wonder how fair it is for young people bent on marriage not to have tough and trying questions, welcome or not, put to them by their elders. What have these elder folk to offer? If they have at least middling good sense and enough affection and respect for the young people, they may not be able to tell anyone whom to marry, but they can say what, if anything, they find faulty in the companionship they are witnessing. A person's parents or shrewd friends can comment less well perhaps on the character of an intended fiancé than on how their own kin or friend shows character in the companionship.

Besides good counsel, there do seem to be a few wise words offered by the tradition to those who want to test their own desire to marry. One concerns time. A wise engagement will generally take a good while of companionship beforehand. And the companionship should involve all sorts of circumstances, not just social amusement. If you are antagonized by your friend's family, find her friends a bit disagreeable, his taste crude, her conversation waning after the first quarter-hour, his interests warming most to things that leave you cold — but are willing to overlook all that because you love him or her so very much and will be able in time to change all that . . . well, you are canoeing toward the falls. But if you don't even allow the kind of time and situations required to know family and friends and tastes and mind, to let boredom or vexation or picky-picky selfishness come to the surface . . . you are heading for the brink, with your eyes closed.

A second cue from the tradition is that sex is a disastrous prelude to marriage. Sexual union means personal union, and if a man and woman have not merged their two lives into one, sex does not tell the truth. Worse, it is so powerful and influential an experience that a continued sexual relationship summons forth from a couple the feelings of being one, while they are still very much two. The feelings are artificially elicited but, like all things counterfeit, they feel like the real thing, especially to one who has not felt the real thing. I can hardly think of a way for two people better to conceal from themselves their true relationship and prospects for marriage than becoming sexually involved. And there is no time in their lives when reliable self-evaluation is more crucial.

* * *

Sex, they say, is a subject upon which Holy Mother Church has been a real scold. Whatever the indiscretions or fixations of her spokesmen, the Church's fundamental under-

standing of sex has been strongly positive. When one is persuaded that sex both requires and confers exquisite love and
fidelity, one is correspondingly cautionary and sharp-tempered
at seeing it frivolously understood and frivolously used. The
Declaration of Independence is a carping and complaining
document precisely because the founding fathers were high
on freedom and had seen too little of it to suit them. Con-
servationists tend to come across to the public as a quarrel-
some lot because there are woodlands and waterways they
know to be precious but are squandered and abused. There
is always worrisome talk from people who value something
highly and mean to see it protected from debasement. Thus
the Church on sex.

The Church has two fairly simple teachings about sex.
The first is that sex is supposed to mean what marriage is
supposed to mean. The second is that sex reveals meaning,
but cannot originate it.

Widespread and well-received is the belief that sex is an
expression of love. Our tradition says otherwise. Not that
one shouldn't or doesn't convey love sexually. But love is not
what makes the sexual exchange truthful; and love alone
cannot prevent its spoilage. There are, after all, countless acts
of love: carrying in the groceries, embracing, or offering one's
kidney for a transplant. None of these is sexual. There may
be many people whom one loves profoundly, yet without
sexual expression. Sex is not the only expression of love, nor
the necessary one. It is not even the greatest: you love your
parents as deeply as anyone but you do not have sex with
them; that does not mean that you love them less than your
spouse. It does mean that your love for them is of a specif-
ically different sort. Sex is appropriate, not simply to exquisite
love, but to a very special kind: pledged love.

What is truthful, proper, distinctive, and defining about
sexual union is that it means: "I take you, for better, for
worse, until death." It means belonging. Of course it is
meant to be an expression of love. Indeed, one will never
live up to it without love. But it is not love which gives it

truth. It must embody the love between two persons who can say to each other, and to no other living person: "I am yours, and all that I have is yours. All that each of us has is not 'mine' or 'yours' but 'ours.'" This is a love-pledge one does not make even to one's children. They may not be loved less, but they are loved differently.

The sharing of the body's privacy is, or ought to be, the sharing of the person's privacy. Only to a spouse has one truly yielded up one's privacy — that which is "mine and no one else's," in person and property. Thus only with a spouse does sex grow to good maturity.

Believing as they do that a couple can and should pledge themselves without reserve or condition, Catholics naturally consider sex a more joyful exchange, having that much more to convey. Believing in the conveyance of an almost unbelievable fidelity, Catholics also naturally see greater loss and greater confusion when sex is put to lesser purposes. This, I suppose, is what has brought on all the cautionary talk.

Someone has said that sex will make a good relationship better, but cannot make a bad one good. This leads to the second point about sex: it is no source of meaning, but a celebration of it. It is derivative. If the meaning is there to be celebrated, there is hardly a better way to do it. When meaning is wanting, not only is the truth not there to be celebrated; a counterfeit is put in its place that makes the truth harder to restore.

A couple makes love by the tens of thousands of gestures of generous, cheerful, humorous, or even dogged service toward one another or family. Love is made by remembering to put antifreeze in the car, by not insisting that one's spouse listen to positively everything that happened since breakfast, by not drinking too much, and by taking the children to the zoo and smacking the one who fed pennies to the seals despite the sign on the wall. So it goes. This is how to *make* love. Couples who do care for each other in this fashion celebrate this sexually and enjoy and are grateful for the profound personal affection sheltered within such workaday services.

If there are failures in these personal bonds of fidelity — and there are always failures — a couple's sexual exchange may reveal them or distract from them, but cannot of itself reverse them, nor can it be quite right itself until they are cured.

Sex cannot give truth to a couple's life together. But neither can it destroy it. Much of the sex research, therapy and counseling done today seems to assume that households are strained to the breaking point by sexual malfunction or ineptitude. Anyone can have sexual difficulties and I suppose that most can be helped out of them. So much the better. But this kind of problem is not at all of the same order or magnitude, say, as alcoholism. The one problem can be borne if other features of the relationship are sound; the other can put the rot into every feature of the relationship. Any couple which imagines its major frustrations and antagonisms come from sexual clumsiness has a real problem, but it isn't pelvic.

Sex is like marriage, and both are like life: they are meant to be mirthful and free and lighthearted. But only those can enjoy them with gusto who ground themselves on commitments that are true and trusted.

*   *   *

Taking children into one's life is a part of good marriage. It is likewise part of good sex. And also of good life. Some say you are never really married until children have arrived. Without going even that far one could say that you are never really married if you have had no appetite for children. If that be true, there are many married people who are not really married.

Many couples do not crave children. This is not because they know we face an overpopulation problem. No matter how aware they are of this problem (and it is a grave problem), men and women make their childbearing decisions from motives more personal, more close to home. Those who tend to act on population worry are wealthy people (and nations) who plead with or pay or sterilize poor people (and nations) not to have so many children because they, the wealthy, know there are things ever so much more important than children, and, besides sharing this insight with the poor, would just as soon not have so many poor kids to pay for. If they were supporting the children of the poor their birth control programs would probably work better.

Couples are chary of children, naturally enough, because children are a burden. A child, unlike a spouse, has to be taken into one's life without one's being able to choose his or her personality. A child claims one's heart and drains one's substance, and then grows up and goes away, without your being sure the child will bring you pride or chagrin. Most obviously, a child costs cash and comfort and convenience.

Children are a burden. A spouse, though, is a burden too. There is a difference: one's partner never seems a burden in the beginning; the bleakness shows later. But one's children seem a burden even before they come. The challenge and the duty and the grace in both is that one be made to grow to love him/her/them so much that serving is no longer burdensome.

Most couples who marry today do not actually refuse children. But many postpone them indefinitely. By "indefinitely" I do not mean that they await the moment when finances and location and careers will make a child feasible, though at the moment they can't quite anticipate when that will be. The indefiniteness often means that conditions are not yet ripe for a child, and the couple really have no clear idea when they will be ripe, or what ripe conditions they are waiting for. They simply don't welcome children yet, and they are waiting to want them. They "need time to get to know each other," to enjoy each other's company. Eventually they will probably have to make a decision to have a child. Some people think it healthier that children come from such clear decisions. The tradition said that, whenever they come, they should come from the original decision to marry, for marriage and childbearing and childrearing were a single summons and a single joy. If, by the time a couple finally consent to have a child, the zest and generosity and openness of their marital decision are waning, and there is a fixed and comfortable round of life into which another comes as an outsider — well, is that healthier?

Other writers in this book say gifted and attracting things about children. I only wish to dwell on the point that children are of marriage, that husband and wife mean household and family. One does have a different love affair with one's children. Out of the sharing of inmost privacy come sons and daughters who share all but that privacy. They need to be given enough privacy and self to take away with them so that they will be able to give it away to another. It cannot be very easy to devote oneself heart and soul to a person, and then see that person turn away and cleave to a stranger. Or to give children gifts which, if truly worthwhile, will be better than they can then appreciate, and perhaps forgotten by the time they've grown enough to appreciate and thank you for them. The most generous gestures of the heart are spent on children who are still growing, and thus always a bit disposed to take those gifts for granted. One has to love very much to raise children. But as I was saying, this is why they are good for people, and why and how they make their parents grow up.

It tends to make one less unselfish by far, to beget and bless and liberate children. Parents who do it well tell me that doing it side-by-side is the best way for husband and wife to get to know each other and appreciate each other.

What is wanted is neither "every family a Trapp Family" with 12+ children filling the happy, boisterous household (it may more likely be boisterous than happy), nor every home producing 2.2 children according to calculated growth needs issued by the Secretary of the Interior. Far better for young couples to crave a child and, having been gifted and grown a bit with it, to make their decisions about another on the strength of what they are learning. To reckon how many children you will have before ever holding your own baby in your hands is not very wise.

Some years back Pope Paul published a letter on birth control which missed the mark. He was trying to argue, to a world unwelcoming to children, that marriage and sex were wrong and selfishly perverted if intentionally closed to child-bearing. This was an assertion which, though hardly fashion-able, was rooted in the tradition, was the sound experience in pastoral practice, and was what people needed to hear. The Pope's timing was courageous, and his principle was sound. It was the more modern application of that principle which went awry. He taught that every single act of sexual inter-course had to be free of any humanly contrived interference with conception, but he did allow that the sequence of inter-course could be harmonized with the rhythm of the monthly fertility cycle so that conception would be unlikely. He called rhythm "natural" and contraception "artificial." His appli-cation would have been more faithful to the tradition, more persuasive, and less disastrous for the Church had he turned it around. It matters less whether any single act of sex be open to conception than whether the entire sequence (not of a month but of a lifetime) of giving and sex and marriage be open to family. Let a couple determine as they will the births of their children, provided they can answer for the pur-pose and outcome and generosity of the whole.

*   *   *

These are a few thoughts about what a man and woman face together if they take each other, for better, for worse, for richer, for poorer, in sickness and in health, until death do them part. If they do it with good and giving hearts, and grow to give more and more, they will sometimes hurt but never be confounded. It is, as Jesus admitted, crazy. But we have faith that if a person have love enough to lay down his or her life for a friend and spouse in marriage, they will both share a kind and quality of love and life which perhaps not even death can part.

2. Our Children Our Greatest Teachers

Eugene S. Geissler

*Friend Husband was 28 when I met him — so I have
no firsthand knowledge of his early years. The person he was
at 28 commanded my immediate interest — there was no
strangeness, no tension — and we were friends from our first
meeting. We were married before his being drafted for service in World War II. Within four months he was overseas
and our first child was almost three years old when he met
her. After the war we settled near Notre Dame. There followed years of teaching and children, farming and children,
building and children, editing and children, writing and
children.*

*These have been good years and the beautiful blessing
from the Marriage Mass, ". . . may you have true friends to
stand by you, both in joy and in sorrow," has been abundantly
present in our lives.*

And we remain friends together.

Jo Geissler

2. Our Children Our Greatest Teachers

This chapter is somewhat in the nature of a family chronicle. It was only gradually that the impact of my children on my education dawned on me. Going back over some things I had written over the years I began to realize what was happening: my children were continually prodding me toward new learning in the art of life. Since I have come to think of this as very important learning, I have come to accord my children their proper place in my education. Thus the title.

I have allowed myself to use some selected observations and insights of the past, but now out of print: on birth, childhood, adolescence. Written in their proper time, close to the experience, they have an immediacy which I couldn't duplicate again. After that I bring the learning up to date. The last 10 years have not only been a continuing education, as is the mode these days, but they have also been climactic. Both the teaching and learning, because of the crisis nature of the times, have reached a new intensity. If by chance it turns out to be the same old education that parents have always received from their children, its special urgency and surprising suddenness may nevertheless be a distinguishing mark for my generation of parents.

* * *

(1945) In the grand cooperation of mankind with God in cocreating human life, the contribution of Adam, the man, is expressed tersely: "And Adam knew Eve his wife." After the initial cooperation in conceiving, the tremendous work of nurturing and sheltering, of housing and shaping the human life in the womb, belongs significantly to Eve, the woman. The husband is on the outside looking in.

Even at the point of accomplishment, at the point of giving birth, of having brought forth, it is Eve, intuitive woman, who utters the great truth of cocreation: "I have gotten a man through God." Eve, the woman, has experienced the process, and Adam, the man, has stood by and waited. The truth she utters she knows firsthand. Intimate knowledge of it comes to Adam only through her.

Yet, the half a line which scripture gives to Adam's part of it is crucial for him: "And Adam knew Eve his wife." Let us not say that scripture meant anything more by the phrase than that Adam had relations with his wife (as it is variously translated now), but let us nevertheless stay with the old word a little: Adam *knew* his wife. Let us suggest that the man's part is really to know his wife.

She is with child. Throughout her pregnancy he tries to know her better and better, because this fulfillment of motherhood in her is a growing and a maturing, a new dimension. With an effort at new insight he tries to understand more and more of what is happening to her as a result of her accepting his knowing her. Except for her yes, the deepest areas of her being would remain closed to him. Except for her yes, there would be no expected child. Instead he has been allowed to know the riches of a woman's warmth and love. The deepest recesses of a woman's heart have been offered to his feeling and knowledge. In many ways, her very intuition has been his teacher. Because he loves her he is sensitive to the details of the process of love and new life within her. Her pregnancy is good news. They share expectations. She has let him know the first signs and the hopes, the physical disturbances and nature's own slow adjustment to this new being within her. She has let him know the first movement of life and the thrill of it. He has known her growing big with child, has sensed the slowing down and the need for patience and attention. He has known the joys — and complications, for while pregnancy and birth are natural things, they are not the normal things. . . .

Giving birth to the child is peculiarly woman's task. She goes "into labor" to bring it forth. There are pain and sorrow, but in them are also great glory and exhilaration. She knows her nearness to God in giving birth and man can only know that from her. If he wants to grow with her he must be sensitive to her. There is unique joy to share. When Christ at the Last Supper was trying to prepare his apostles for what was shortly to come — his suffering, death and resurrection — he called forth this very situation in the life of woman as a parallel: "A woman about to give birth has sorrow, because her hour is come. But when she has brought forth the child, she no longer remembers the anguish for her joy that a man (woman) is born into the world."

The birth of a child is a growing and maturing time for both husband and wife. It *is* a miracle and they are part of it. The woman is the main actress in the drama and the husband, by entering into a supporting and appreciative role, open to what is going on, can share in one of the most meaningful and satisfying events this world has to offer man.

It is a good sign of the times — partly through the young people's insistence — that the husband can be with his wife during the delivery. My wife and I protested for years not being able to be together for the birth of our children. Those who can, have that much more to share for the rest of their lives — not some small experience on the periphery of life, but a real and central experience of sorrow, joy, and the nearness of God.

*   *   *

(1950) In our own experience, which goes some time back to be sure, the father "inherited" the old baby when the new baby came along. No two people were ever so made for each other's pure enjoyment as father and his new inheritance. The inheriting was not a formal process, of course, but just by the nature of things these two began to gravitate toward each other, the father replacing the mother at many points.

Nature intended that the father should be eased into his offspring. A mother's love is never so motherly as when the child is most new, most fragile, most helpless and most dependent on her. The father's love for his child, deep as it might be, awaits more or less the time of the baby's first walking to assert and demonstrate itself. There is a sense in which a mother is born and not made — born, if not before, then with the birth of her child. But a father does not experience but only knows that he is a father and grows into or up to his fatherhood only gradually. So that a father is more made than born. An inexperienced father handling an infant or even just holding it can look very awkward indeed. A mother, no matter how young and new, is not without a certain innate finesse in the matter.

This making of the father is a two-way street — the while he is making himself into a father, he is also being made into a father. To begin with, he is just a man with his own personality to which his fatherhood adds a new and, depending on his ways, maybe a revolutionary note. In some instances it doesn't require much change or effort to be a father, i.e., a "good father"; in another instance, it may require deep-seated changes. It is not so much a matter of personality because different kinds of personalities can all make good, though different fathers; it is more a matter of development, a matter of realizing the fatherhood within oneself. Even more is it a matter of being sensitive to the needs, the demands, the exigencies, the possibilities, the talents, the potentialities of his new inheritance. Except perhaps in his marriage, a man will never again have as many opportunities and natural motives, so many reminders and incentives, to correct and perfect himself, to be what he should be, as on this two-way street between father and child.

For, a father should know, or come to know, that while the child learns indeed many things from him — even to the point of imitating him in small ways and mannerisms — the child has also something to "teach": "Unless you become as little children, you shall not enter the kingdom of heaven." Or as it says in a poem:

> Or did she mean that I might learn from him?
> A son can teach a father what he should have been.

It is not merely that a father begins gradually to realize what it means to be a father, or what duties or what joys go with being a father, and to refashion himself accordingly, even changing his ways. This is certainly growing up to fatherhood. But more important than that, having learned to be a father to his child, he has at the same time learned how to be a child of God, the Father of us all.

A whole new area of understanding now opens up to him for the first time. It is the closing of the circle between his own father, himself and his child, the closing of the circle of his experience. Or one might say that he is now in the center and for the first time can see full circle. From the center of the circle, he begins slowly to know and comprehend both his role as a father and his role as a son. He begins to know and understand what he never knew and understood before: all the problems, efforts, nuances, heartaches, of the paternal-filial relation. What a revelation and what learning it is! What food for thought and meditation! What source of appreciation, purification and even repentance! Now he knows what he should have been, what he still should be in relation to God.

God will make all things right for those who learn to know and love him. To have come to know oneself, one's life, one's own history, and to have evaluated it in perspective before God — to see the omissions and to admit the imperfections is still to be growing up to fatherhood. This time to the fatherhood of God. It is never too late. The opportunity let slip by, the failures suffered, the mistakes made, the duties left undone, even the sins committed — and now insight and sorrow. . . . Seen in its entirety as God sees it — God in whom there is no time — the change of heart has not gone unheeded; in fact, has already been taken into consideration.

*   *   *

(1955) There are other things, too, a man never understands until he is himself a father — his own parents, for instance, and in a way all those who have gone before.

Being a father is to take for a while the main part in the drama of the generations. It is to be (with mother) in the center of the stage of life between children and grandparents — the busy and burdened man of the world between the ages of careless freedom and leisurely reflection.

Once upon a time, this father took his five oldest children with him to the grave of his parents in the country cemetery behind the country church and school that were so much a part of his life as a boy. He used to play there — tag, prisoner's base, baseball, of course, and something called "shinny," with a stick and battered tin can — between the church and the cemetery, scarcely giving a thought in all those years to the dead. His own father was among them and later his mother, too; an uncle killed in the woods, an aunt dead in the flush of womanhood; and then his grandparents — long-lived people.

Today he read the family names on a hundred family lots and, with a new kind of care and concern, remembered them all; they were all familiar names, the heritage of his boyhood, the people he grew up with, the only people in life who really knew him from young up, and he them.

Today he had an inkling of his vocation of father. He stood, the middleman between his own children beside him and his parents dead in their graves. He stood in the middle generation of the world between the past and the future — and standing there he understood himself in the full stature of life between the young and the old.

It is the center of the stage and, in the drama of the generations, a man as father holds it but a little while. It is an important position, a responsible mission, a true vocation. It means to carry for a while the load and the hope of the world, to forge a link in the human chain from Adam forward to God, to pass on enriched what has been received, to give life, to teach, to start those dependent on him on the way to eternal salvation.

Only so can a father pass on in peace.

*   *   *

(1960) During the first six or seven years children belong as never again to their parents. During these years they shape them in the greatest possible freedom, according to the way they want and according to the way parents themselves are. The home is the great influence — and if parents make the effort, the only real influence. For what they are at six or seven is what their parents have made them by what they have given them. All the important things have been, or could have been, under their control.

The situation changes a little from six or seven to 12 or 14, but not too much. There is a great mental awakening with the coming of the "age of reason," but home remains the great influence. It is true that it is not the only influence, by any means, but the most important influence, for everything in the nature of children of this age still centers in the home and around the parents, and in the neighborhood where the home casts a benign shadow, and if beyond the neighborhood, then always in touch with home. Emotionally children of this age are content with this, and the security of home is sweet to them and, granting the basic things such as the love of father and mother, they are much more delight than worry, extremely compensating, indeed a great pleasure — no big problems, no deep misunderstandings, a peaceful time of life. In a way, these are children at their best.

I have come to believe that the greatest teachers in our lives are our children. It is true that they don't teach us much in the way of practical or scientific knowledge, but they are the source at various stages of their lives of a considerable teaching through the human insights they occasion.

Consider, for instance, the little child sitting on his father's lap. He sits there with an integrity all his own: a totality of innocent dependence, one person on another. The father is both the depended on and the dependent one, and he learns from this little child how slowly man grows and with what pains the human race itself moves forward only slowly. Is this a small thing to have learned? How differently than before will this man now view the future, other human beings, and the world around him? (The unknown author of the *Desiderata* may well have been a father who had just taken a long look at his child.)

Or consider, for instance, the grown child who during the ages of nine to 12 achieves as a child a beautiful maturity of his own. For there is such a thing as a grown-up child who in his maturity achieves a wholeness and completeness that teaches a father right then and there what he should be here and now. What does this mature child teach by his example and by what he is? (And recall how Jesus put a child in their midst as a model.)

A sense of openness and wonder, a sense of security with himself, a curiosity about life and an ease with living it, a simplicity before God and a trust of others, a willingness to help, to contribute and to fit in, a sense of fairness which knows justice and sympathy, and sometimes a sense of unselfishness and even sacrifice. Does anyone think that living in a house over a period of years with three or four such people does not humanize man?

On top of it all, what really touches the soft growth core of the human being that we all are at the center is that these nice people do really love their grumpy fathers. Speaking of children, it is as nine-year-old Margaret said in a little poem about stars: "Stars are very big but we see them small."

The years of childhood are good years, and yet they end up imperfectly. Parents weren't the great masters of fate and shapers of destiny that they thought they were. One day the sigh of a new wind disturbs their euphoria. At the age of 12 Jesus is lost in the Temple and explains that it is because he must be about "his Father's business." He asks, a bit defiantly: "Why did you look for me?"

Jesus is not untypical in feeling and expressing a desire for growing up and reaching beyond. In a way, it was a notice that childhood had come to an end. It gave Mary something else to ponder in her heart, another stage in her own maturing. Parents learn many things from their children.

The children begin to knock, filled with a new curiosity for life, on the doors of the world — especially the world within themselves. Almost too suddenly they begin to turn against home and to question it; they rebel and fume and sputter and do strange things on the misty flats between dependence and independence. In a way they get lost and find it hard to "return to Nazareth." (I think the biblical story covering this time of Jesus leaves some things unsaid.)

Obviously, it is a growing-up time for children who must now begin to find their own selves and live their own lives. But it is a growing-up time for parents too. Lightning is striking at the deepest roots of selfishness: they have to "give up" their children. Here before them lies the world of sacrifice, stripped cleaner than ever before. The time has come to put away all the immature and imperfect ways of loving their children which are so easily part of young family life when children in their dependence are emotionally satisfying. Now comes the time of giving out of sheer and unalloyed love because love is so little returned — and the recipients of it so demanding, so heedless and so self-centered. It is a time of heartaches, misunderstandings, worries, and probably suffering as well. The message to parents is "to go up higher." They are deeply involved with these lives and need to hold fast to the duties of their commitment more than ever: the children need them as a point of stability and a point of return.

*   *   *

(1965) After having seen six children through adolescence I had occasion to reflect about what I called positively at the time: "A Father's Second Chance" (*There Is a Season,* Ave Maria Press, 1969). It went like this:

As his teenagers try to come to terms with the world and the meaning of life for the first time, a father has to face the issues of life a second time. In a way, it is also his second chance.

It is possible to miss the second chance even more easily than the first one because the older we are the thicker is the armor of protection that we build around ourselves. Also, there is always some way, until death, of evading the issues, of jumping on the merry-go-round, of living life on the surface, of hiding. There are enough gadgets and distractions around these days to make playing at escape rather easy and endless, though obviously it doesn't lead to happiness and, if one may say so, not to reality either. And where the reality is, there the meaning also is.

Confronted by himself, by the world, and by the meaning of life during his own adolescence, a person does normally achieve a measure of maturity and a measure of adulthood. Yet, both of these things I see now as relative and never very perfect at all. There is always at least a little, if not a lot more, maturity to achieve. There is always something to be added or to be refined about one's attitude toward life and one's grasp of the meaning of life. Maturity is not a static state, a high plateau with no place else to go. It too is subject to the dynamism of change. Exposed a second time to searching and deciphering the meaning of life with his teenagers, a father may well be challenged to go up higher and to see better.

If he stays close enough and open enough to his teenagers the questions they ask in their searching can help him expose the phoniness in the world he helped shape and in the life he is living. Even fathers are living out a lot of compromise with mammon and with the world which may have crept in while they were not looking but which can now stand a second look through the uncompromising eyes of teenagers, through whom he is confronting human life anew.

Not only are fathers, of all people, the most exposed, but as Péguy has said, because they are exposed, fathers are of all people the most vulnerable. This exposure, this vulnerability, is very elusive as an insight unless one is a father. When I first read it in Péguy, it didn't touch me very deeply — though I remembered it — whereas now I feel I might have thought of it myself. The father is exposed to all the vicissitudes of life through his children, and there are many situations in which he is as helpless as they are and can only suffer with them. He is exposed to many situations in which, during their adolescence, he is in the battle of growing up with them and can only feel with them since he cannot do for them. He faces with them the big questions of life from their point of view, not knowing all the answers at all. He shares their doubts, some of their confusion, even some of their rebellion. For others the problem is not the same; they bring something else to it. In fact, they can even walk away from it.

Because of his exposure a father is vulnerable for several reasons. He is vulnerable first of all because for him there is no running away. He is, of all people, directly involved and there is no wiggling out of it even when there is no solution. He has taken on a burden of human beings personally, and from this burden there is no justified escape. He once was a free man who could ride off on a horse in any direction. He could tell most any situation to go to hell. But not anymore.

He is vulnerable, too, because now he has to listen and let the outside world into his house. This is especially true when his children are bungling forward toward independence. A man could almost go from his own adolescence to his death on the same set of principles and values — good, bad, or indifferent — that he achieved in the first stage of maturity, if he were not vulnerable as a father.

I really think that this exposure and vulnerability can

be a kind of salvation, can lead to growth, can add a new dimension. Imagine having to subject cherished principles you have come to live by, and even to swear by, to being questioned. Why? Your very life manifests in a kind of epiphany what the meaning of success is! What you stand for, and have stood for since coming to grips with reality during your own adolescence is almost a personification of the true meaning of life! But is it?

Some people can dismiss the questions because they have all the answers, but a father has a more difficult time than others dismissing them because they come to him from "his own flesh and blood." Not only that: if he does not listen and accept that the questions have value, he cannot help those who have need of his help. And so he asks himself anew: What are the things that are important in life? What is success? What am I here for? Where did I come from? Where am I going? Is there a God? And if there is, how do I love him? Am I my brother's keeper? Who was Christ? Where is he today? What is the meaning of human life in a world threatened with too much life?

The vulnerability, if nothing else, tends to set up a dialogue between a father and his children, between the ever-changing new world of the son and the vanishing world of the father, between the hard line a man is prone to take in shaping the world scientifically and efficiently and the soft human touch of the daughter, serious about not merely doing something but being somebody fully human.

*   *   *

(1970) It has become a theme of my life that my greatest teachers have been my children. I didn't arrive at this suddenly but only gradually over the years. I think I really knew what I was saying when I spoke of it as a "father's second chance" at the age of 50. Not all the learning has been easy and painless.

In the 10 years following, the world around me has changed so much that what seemed at first like a great chasm opened up between the father and the children. The rebellion of youth has been no ordinary one. They followed young leaders who cut off the heads of their fathers and danced to young and reckless drummers. Their generation has actually been called "a generation without fathers," and the phenomenon has been called "the generation gap." The old words of "growing up," "becoming independent," "leaving home," gave way to words like "doing your own thing," "playing it cool," and "hanging loose."

Parents who had children in college in the late 60's and early 70's will immediately understand what I am saying. So many things that together we had held sacred in the areas of religion and morality were tossed aside and the values substituted for them were from another world. The new gods were freedom and honesty, one's own feelings and privacy, one's own experience and experimentation — typical adolescent gods in whose names drugs and thrills, vulgarity and pornography, noncommitment and fornication, trial marriage and adultery, homosexuality and even abortion . . . could be justified. All these things were, at the same time, an assault on the values of Christian marriage and the religion that stood for them.

As parents we thought we were open to what our children wanted to do with their lives, but somehow we hadn't included the possibilities of sin and apostasy. Nevertheless, we have come to understand that the "student revolution" had a good side as well, and I insist to myself that we cannot know yet all the good it will have prompted and put into motion by its single-minded assault on conventional beliefs. It will be a long time before the attacks on the long-established and painstakingly built-up values of Christian marriage and family life will have been sifted through, and new and acceptable values, purified and graced, will have taken their place. There are signs of hope and optimism. The Spirit of God is very active upon the face of the earth. The words of Paul to the Romans come to mind: "Where sin increased, grace abounded all the more."

However, I remember well the day and the hour when the world the parents had so carefully built up came down around their ears. It had to be Christmastime when everybody was home. The family atmosphere was unsettled and uneasy. Tensions were in the air. Divisions and anxieties brooded underneath. And then it happened. It was like a ship hitting an iceberg. Not that much showed above the surface, but for the parents it was enough to know that they had been hit hard and that the waters were full of danger.

What happened? Let me say simply that some of our college-age children (we had four in colleges at the time) had gone over to living and preaching another gospel. I couch the happening in terms of "another gospel" because anything less would not have affected the parents the same way. Loyalties became divided, family unity was gone. The middle family especially was caught in between. We were such a big family for that to happen to and to this day even the influence of the older on the younger children is an unsolvable problem. Talk about a whole new area of life opening up when a child is born to a couple! Talk about learning virtues from children in the maturity of their childhood! Talk about reevaluating your philosophy of life when your children go through their adolescence!

What is there to be learned from being crucified? First of all, forgiveness. The need to forgive and to be forgiven becomes the single most important element in healing the broken relationships. It becomes necessary not only to forgive but to forget. It might begin on the part of parents with Jesus' own words: "Father, forgive them for they know not what they do." They really don't know what they are doing to their parents. Nor is it that one-sided. Parents can't dismiss what has happened by blaming it entirely on others. Parents find that they made mistakes. God in his mercy might even reveal their sins to them, and then they can ask forgiveness most sincerely of both God and their children. To forgive is divine and in that divinity there is great power to heal and to make whole again.

Secondly, with suffering and helplessness there comes a new dependence on God. In fact, dependence on God emerges as the true mark of a child of God. It isn't only that in desperation parents call upon God for help and are indeed heard by God as the Lord says. It is a new relationship with God. Perhaps faith and hope had become clouded over by their own talents and abilities, their own system and method. It has resulted for us in a new way of praying, in a new faith and hope founded on God's plan for each of the parents and children alike. It is a new call to faith in God's seed planted in baptism, in God's gift of the Spirit in confirmation, in God's love in the Eucharist. Recall Jesus saying to the Father: "I have not lost one of these you have given to me." We have certainly given each child to him and he will deal with each in his good time. And oh, it is a call to patience. Waiting on God is a call to great patience.

Thirdly, in the first flush of catastrophe, my wife and I, after so many years of trusting each other's wisdom in dealing with the children, entertained doubts about each other's methods. We became introspective, made judgments and blamed each other for what had happened. I had been too permissive, she said; she had been too strict, I said. It ended up in those trying times to be the worst division of all and showed up the long fingers of sin. It was a dark night, a longer and darker night than when our Annie died prematurely in the midst of us.

But God is good, and there came a new dawn for the husband and wife relationship. Out of the darkness came a new and purer light, and I am reminded of the days when we first loved each other and everything was pristine-beautiful between us. Through some miracle of grace it is so again, only richer and more knowledgeable. God still loves two only children of his who came before him in marriage and asked for his blessing. He has blessed us once again. Our newfound dependence on him has turned our faces toward each other in a new way. Perhaps we have, by experience of collapse, been emancipated from the burden of saving our children by

ourselves. Yes, I think so. We have been freed to love each
other again as two in one and one in the Lord. Our covenant
with God does not extend to our children. God has no grandchildren, it is said. He deals with each as his son or daughter.
What a relief!

Finally, part of this last point is the realization and
acceptance of the total otherness of even our own children.
The roots of this otherness go back to the uniqueness of each
child in the image of God. It derives from God's separate love
for each of his children. Each one is totally other in his plan
and his love.

It is no easy thing for parents really to accept this
"strangeness" in each of their children, to free them once and
for all into the hand of God who is their real father and
mother, and before whom we are equals in his love, one no
more than the other, and each totally other in his relationship
with God. We, parents and children, had arrived at the point
where being together depended on our being separate human
beings united, if at all, by a common father-God who had
affirmed each of us singly by his first and total love of each
of us. In one way or another this jealous God and supreme
Lover divides us from each other to unite us again in himself.
This is just beginning to happen.

*   *   *

(1975) The final word, the last in this family litany, is
compassion. To think that I might have died without really
knowing what the word means. Thanks to my children, I
didn't.

As I reflect on what I have written here and elsewhere
on family life the word compassion does not come to me when
I add up all the intimacies, joys and funny little things that
happen in a house full of children. Nor does it come to my
mind when I think of the moments of exhilaration and the
warm and happy days of life shared abundantly with one
another. Nor even in those rare flashes of insight and inspiration that, like slivers of light, illuminate life lived from day to
day in a home. I am aware that I have preferred for many

years to write pleasantly about these pleasant happenings.

No, the word compassion has come to me only lately since I have begun to reap some of the pain and sorrow that prosper so well in the soil of a father's vulnerability and have, strangely enough, been willing to talk about it. Suffering shared is an open door to compassion. It is not easy, if possible at all, to suffer with others without having first suffered oneself. Even then the suffering has not only to be embraced and accepted but there has to be the willingness to share it at the proper time and in the proper manner with others. So, it is when I add up the not-so-pleasant things, the meaning of the sad events and the weight of tragedy, the frustrations and disillusionments, the irreconcilable differences and the unsolvable problems, the sometimes helplessness and hopelessness, the mistakes and the failures of family life that I begin to think of compassion.

My wife has remarked that it is only since people know what has happened to us, or that it has happened to us too, that people come to her with their troubles in these troubled times. She listens and shares, and what is going on between the two sufferers is compassion. It is like I said one day: "We have finally joined the human race." It is like an incarnation and might very well be the beginning of being more Christlike.

One never knows what the day will bring. Much less does one know what marriage and family will bring. Sometimes I feel like the old man beside the railroad tracks watching the empties coming back — except that I am not that man. Nor is any father who has given himself over to his tasks and duties that man. It is because we have been emptied out that our hearts can be full of compassion for others. Emptiness is the common denominator of a brooding, suffering world. Paradoxically, those with compassion are not empty long.

Compassion signifies a special kind of growth and learning that reaches beyond one's own family. It is part of the necessary exchange to make humanity whole. It is the touch that heals other people's children. For in this strange exchange

among suffering persons, it is possible to do for others what
you can't do for yourself, and to do for other people's children
what you can't do for your own.

I see only two ways to compassion. The natural way is
through family life, through the vulnerability of loving,
through the kind of commitment to loved ones that ends in
suffering with others their miseries and griefs. The other way,
more directly in imitation of Christ, is through the Spirit of
Christ given to us in faith, in baptism, scripture . . . which
enables us to see Christ in every other who needs our help
and healing. Perhaps for Christians the two are ultimately
the same, for Paul's word to husbands was in the same terms:
"Love your wives in the same way that Christ loved the
church and gave his life for it."

In our confused and convoluted, twisted and fragmented
world, we are confronted daily with those who are in need
of our compassion. It is necessary only to be aware and capable of compassion. From the other side, we are also confronted with a multitude of opportunities for learning compassion. It seems to me that the whole world of compassion
is open to all of us because of our "family" connections. We
all have fathers and mothers, all but a few of us have brothers
and sisters, most of us have sons and daughters — and grandparents and some of us even grandchildren. On the natural
level our common denominator for compassion is the network
of these family connections, and the measure of our compassion is related to our involvement, conscious and aware,
in sufferings of the family of man available through these
family relationships. The most intense of these and therefore
the most fruitful for learning compassion are at the same
time the most common: those between parents and children.

In my office on a bulletin board I have posted some pictures out of the news. Not many, but having thought of them
right now I asked myself why those pictures attracted me and
why I put them up. One is a picture of a young Nicaraguan
mother pressing her small child to her neck and shoulder.
Her face is sober-sad, and the sufferings of the past and future

lie across her countenance. It is a close-up, but you can visualize her standing among the ruins of the earthquake and you know her vulnerability and suffering because you too are a father or mother.

Another picture is an airport shot of a war prisoner's return home to his family. He is shown from the back with his arms wide but in subdued gesture open to receive his family, sons and daughters and wife, rushing toward him. Their hearts are full of joy and the camera seems to have caught all six of them with their feet off the ground. You are happy for them, but if tears come to your eyes, it is because you are aware of the poignant family suffering and anxiety that have gone before and are over now for a little while.

A third picture, oddly enough, is the center spread of an issue of the FBI magazine: a "Wanted" poster of William and Emily Harris and Patty Hearst — aliases, front and side pictures, different disguises, "must be considered dangerous" warnings, and all. I might have put it up for just a curiosity, but I might also have seen in it a personification of the generation-gap children, victims themselves of having cut off the heads of their fathers. But as a father who has been part of the sufferings inherent in something similar, I understand the ambivalence of the situation and my heart is capable of going out in compassion to father and mother and children — whether rich or poor, guilty or innocent — because it might just as easily, so very easily, have been me and mine.

*   *   *

(1977) As long as life lasts, a family chronicle remains unfinished, as does the learning. With every day and decade there is more to write. Optimistically, I predict that the next entry in this chronicle will be a happy one. Something good has begun to happen and I hope that the happy tomorrow I predict is for every other family as well, especially for those with whom I have shared a sometimes not-so-happy yesterday.

In another sense, a family chronicle has no ending at all. We ourselves are each part of something longer than our lives.

In my time I have learned from my children at the same time they have learned from me what my father and I have learned in a previous time from each other. In a short while it is my children's turn.

Yet each of us contributes something unique because we are unique. Most of what we learn from life is never written down but handed on and worked over in a myriad of ways by parents and children together. The happy tomorrow has something to do with the generation without fathers knowing once again their fathers, and the fathers their children. For inevitably we walk together in the greatest of human adventures: finding our way to God.

3. Women and Marriage Today

Sally Cunneen

Sally McDevitt Cunneen grew up in Providence, Rhode Island, developing a love for the ocean, Portuguese sweet bread, and amateur dramatics. Despite the rigors of St. Sebastian's elementary school, she at one time conceived her vocation to be that of secretary to the pope. Now that the secularizing influences of Classical High School, Smith College, the University of Toronto, and Teachers College (Columbia) have done their work, she would settle for an opportunity to give a folk song recital at the Vatican, accompanying herself on the dulcimer.

Although she is prone to see the darker possibilities of life when her husband is driving, she has a delicious sense of humor which always manages to triumph, even over nagging pains caused by allergies and near despair over the constant household disorder due to unfinished editorial work being left in every room. She is an infectious teacher, whose continuing education classes at Rockland Community College often run overtime as group discussion generates its own momentum. She complains because she has no time to write, but always puts her husband, sons and friends first. Her husband, however, still smarting from frequent defeats in tennis, wants to know, now that she has finished the proofs for the next issue of Cross Currents, *corrected all her freshman papers, sketched out a report for an ecumenical meeting, completed another chapter of her dissertation on Iris Murdoch, helped youngest son Paul with his German assignment, and prepared beef Stroganoff for visitors who will be arriving in a few hours, why couldn't she dash off a short story before they come, instead of copping out by taking a nap.*

Joseph Cunneen

3. Women and Marriage Today

To speak of marriage after 26 surprising years of it, with the same man, is almost as difficult as to speak of being alive, or a woman, or an American; the subject is endless and my attitude might be considered self-serving. So I will begin by confessing that when I married, I was not at all sure I approved of "marriage" as distinct from the man with whom I had chosen to spend my life. At the time I was against everything structural and "formal," thinking it meant empty or oppressive forms, insincerity, impersonality. I wanted to have and to receive total commitment in an authentically personal way. For my mother's sake I went through the ceremonies, from being given away to silver bells on top of the wedding cake, but did I accept the institution of marriage? I have never been able to face the question squarely until the present time, and I would like to try to tell you why.

As a child I had observed a mysterious phenomenon: lively young women who sometimes sledded and played ball with us younger children on the hills and streets of Providence seemed to disappear mysteriously as they reached their late teens. They were seen later only through the announcement of their engagements in the *Journal*. Houses had apparently

swallowed them up and away from the beauties of the outside world. The behavior of these young women had the effect
on me of a cautionary tale. I could not help but be suspicious
of anything that threatened to impose such limitations on my
future. I did not talk about these things; my attitudes were
scarcely formed. But added to the largely "formal" relationships I had seen among most married couples, my subterranean feelings meant that I could not *assume* I would marry,
though clearly I had no attraction whatsoever to the celibate
life.

In my small, excellent public high school I encountered
a few admirable single women teachers, yet realized they were
considered "characters." Two or three other marvelous women
I knew were either widows or separated from their husbands.
My best friend and I considered the length and breadth of
the injustice that seemed so to limit the opportunities available to spirited women as we simultaneously surveyed the
male field on the floor at dancing class, each of us praying
that no young man more than two inches shorter than we
would ask us for the next dance.

To complicate matters further, I had my mother's case
to consider. A talented and lovely woman, she had greatly
desired children and made us feel wanted and loved. She was
in every obvious way the kind of mother anyone would have
chosen except in one: she did not respect herself enough because, despite a husband who thoroughly lived his conviction
that women were the fully equal partners of men, the social
patterns of the community did not expect or encourage women
to contribute except in very limited ways. And so my
mother — who looked like Loretta Young, was a keen business woman, played the piano superbly, could knit sweaters,
crochet dresses and hook rugs as well as speak in three languages — did not feel at ease with herself because she found
no way to relate to the larger world through her talents. Her
growing sense of insufficiency made us undervalue her as we
grew into adolescence, and this in turn created further defensiveness on her part, more intense concentration on home

activities (Don't go out! *I* can make you a Baked Alaska!) and children (I want you to be *successful!*), so that we felt smothered.

When I married I felt sure that my understanding of the problems I might face would be sufficient protection against them. I did not then know the limits of intellectual awareness. Nor did I realize that marriage was a leap of faith despite the mutual suitability and commitment of the partners, and an unpredictable crucible of experience. Taking thought about it beforehand is as helpful a preparation for marriage as it is for waterskiing. Most of us are forced, under the unbelievable pressure of running a home and raising children, to sort out all the ragtag attitudes to sex, male-female roles, and children that we inherited from our own families, our churches and the crazy quilt of social and commercial influences we call our culture. I don't know what would have prepared me: perhaps growing up in a larger family, having had to work harder and earlier for a living, or having had the physical stamina of an Olympic athlete. Unfortunately, I had loved books and solitude, had a weak back and allergies, and in a few years found myself, against my will, falling into my mother's pattern of losing self-esteem and increasing emotional demands on my family.

*   *   *

It was no surprise to me when Betty Friedan's book about the housewife's "problem that has no name" appeared and women began to question in public the institution which church and society had long told them was instituted largely for their benefit. And if it was thought at first that only the feelings of middle-class women with time on their hands were being aired, their voices were soon joined by others from varied ethnic, religious and class groups. Tillie Olsen's story, "I Stand Here Ironing," reveals the inner torment of a mother who knows she has not given her firstborn daughter the love she needed; the mother has just received a note from the now teenage daughter's teacher, asking for help in understanding this difficult child:

I will never total it all. I will never come in to say:
She was a child seldom smiled at. Her father left
me before she was a year old. I had to work her
first six years when there was work, or I sent her
home and to his relatives. . . . She was a child of
anxious, not proud, love. We were poor and could
not afford for her the soil of easy growth. I was a
young mother, I was a distracted mother. There
were the other children pushing up, demanding . . : . My wisdom came too late. She has much
to her and probably nothing will come of it. . . .
    Let her be. So all that is in her will not
bloom — but in how many does it? (*Tell Me a
Riddle,* Dell, 1961).

Olsen raises the question again from the girl-child's point
of view in her autobiographical novel, *Yonnondio From the
Thirties.* Moving from mining town to bleak farm to a home
near the filthy Chicago stockyards, the girl sees her mother's
imaginative self flicker and disappear except for one brief
afternoon when they visit the unfamiliar suburbs to gather
dandelion greens for dinner. Exhausted, they sit down on the
grass and the mother sings.

A fragile old remembered comfort streamed from
the stroking fingers into Mazie, gathered to some
shy bliss that shone despairingly over suppurating
hurt and want and fear and shamings — the harm
of years. . . . The fingers stroked, spun a web, co-
cooned Mazie into happiness and intactness and
selfness. Soft wove the bliss round hurt and fear
and want and shame — the old worn fragile bliss,
a new frail selfness bliss, healing, transforming. Up
from the grasses, from the earth, from the broad
tree trunk at their back, latent life streamed and
seeded. The air and self shone boundless. . . .
    "I'm hungry," Ben said.
    "Watch me jump," Jimmie called imperi-
ously. "Momma, Mazie, watch. You're not watching!"

The wind shifted, blew packing house. Something whirred, severed, sank. A tremble of complicity ran through Mazie's body; with both hands she tethered her mother's hand, to keep it, stroking, stroking. Too late. *Between a breath, between a heartbeat, the weight settled, the bounds reclaimed* (Dell, 1974).

Tillie Olsen's lyrical stories remind us that for most men and women until quite recently, economic and biological necessity has limited the potential rewards of marriage. In the European Middle Ages and the Renaissance, women were married without their consent, bore children early and often, and they as well as the majority of their offspring died young. But because children were economically and socially valuable, both men and women could respect themselves and one another throughout lives of common struggle and deprivation. Among the wealthy, marriage was a property settlement for the benefit of the families involved. The romantic love so much a part of our literature and assumptions arose outside of marriage among those wealthy enough to enjoy the leisure necessary for its cultivation.

With the rise of the middle class and its gathering in urban centers, by the 18th century some romance had begun to attach itself to a marital state which increasingly allowed personal choice to both partners. Rousseau spoke of these new personal satisfactions in *Emile* when he praised marriage as "a love founded on esteem which will last with life itself, on virtues which will not fade with fading beauty, on fitness of character which gives a charm to intercourse, and prolongs to old age the delights of early love." Most of these rewards, however, were clearly restricted to husbands, while wives were merely restricted. Emile's chosen bride, Sophie, for instance, is given a limited education to prepare her for the rigors of perfect housemanship and the joys of companionship with her farmer-husband. Rousseau provides historical precedent:

When the Greek women married, they disappeared from public life; within the four walls of their home

they devoted themselves to the care of their household and family. This is the mode of life prescribed
for women alike by nature and reason.

As a clincher he adds:

This habitual restraint produces a docility which
woman requires all her life long, for she will always
be in subjection to a man, or to man's judgment,
and she will never be free to set her own opinion
above his.

Jane Austen's novels reveal that little had changed for
19th-century English women: bagging a man with enough
pounds a year was still the only game in town. Yet the fact
that the single Jane Austen has given us her beautifully clear
human portraits of English middle-class life in the Napoleonic
era should be proof enough of the wastefulness of such social
limitations for women. How lucky we are that Jane (like
many other spunky aunts and sisters through the centuries)
persisted and was supported by her affectionate family in what
was then most irregular behavior.

In 1905 that sensitive critic of American progress, Henry
Adams (*The Education of Henry Adams*), pointed out that
an undervaluation of feminine powers and possibilities was
one of the chief causes of an increasing social malaise. Henry
Adams recorded "a general law of experience — no woman
had ever driven him wrong; no man had ever driven him
right." Yet he saw women suppressing their powers and following their men rather than their instincts, even though they
were obviously discontented with these men. He grimly pre-
dicted an American future in which the women, continuing
on this course, would "marry machinery" like their men. He
was speaking, I believe, of the cultural separation that occurred in American life as a factor in its emergence as a major
technological power. Personal, "feminine" values — and
women — were relegated to the private sphere while aggressive "masculine" values — and men — dominated public life.

When I turned on the radio this morning and heard a satin-smooth voice suggest "There must be 50 ways to leave your lover!" then picked up the *Times* and saw a book ad promising to turn women on with 39 sex fantasies "based on extensive research," I was reminded how prophetic Adams had been. We all seem threatened today with reduction to the machines we have espoused. In our society children are no longer an asset or even allies. In his *Culture Against Man* anthropologist Jules Henry describes the extent to which money-market values have intruded into the sanctuary of the American home: man and wife now vie for the affections of the children, children compete with adults for scarce jobs, and mental illness thrives amid the increased tension. But the technology that determines so much of our way of life is at least potentially more subject to human control than were the natural forces that determined the lives of primitive peoples. Modern technology has made it possible to have sex and not to have children. It has improved sanitation, prevented disease, and peopled the globe with older men and women, although it has not yet sufficiently increased food supplies. Despite the fact that we do not really control these large-scale developments, our marriage to machines has at least brought with it some choice as to what we might do with our lives, and especially with our marriages.

Those who see women's questioning of traditional marriage or women's changed consciousness in general as the cause of our current increase in divorces, single-parent families and general moral decay are confusing cause with symptom and even with possible solution. Freed from the inexorability of childbearing, women are raising questions about the purpose and quality of life. Now that the repression of their instincts and personal values which Henry Adams recorded is breaking up, we should look carefully as he did at the connection between their revelations and possible new directions for marriage as well as for our technological society. Of course, the same widespread technological changes that have enabled women to realize they have options in life-style have done the same for men, who are also rethinking the nature and quality of their roles and relationships. This reexamination is related and mutually constructive. I concentrate here on women's experience because I am more familiar with it.

*   *   *

I have chosen three significant areas of widespread feminine disillusionment that ultimately lend themselves to a positive reenvisioning of marriage. The first is the yawning disparity between the reality of married life and the romantic notions we have of it. Peter Berger writes:

> In Western countries, and especially in America, it is assumed that men and women marry because they are in love. There is a broadly based popular mythology about the character of love as a violent, irresistible emotion that strikes where it will, a mystery that is the goal of most young people and often of the not-so-young as well. As soon as one investigates, however, which people actually marry each other, one finds that the lightning-shaft of Cupid seems to be guided rather strongly within very definite channels of class, income, education, racial and religious background. If one then investigates a little further into the behavior that is engaged in prior to marriage under the rather misleading euphemism of "courtship," one finds channels of interaction that are often rigid to the point of ritual. The suspicion begins to dawn on one that, most of the time, it is not so much the emotion of love that creates a certain kind of relationship, but that carefully predefined and often planned relationships eventually generate the desired emotion. (*Invitation to Sociology,* Doubleday, 1963).

The reason this illusion is bad is not that a wife expects to lie forever enthroned on a chaise longue in harem pajamas as she breathlessly awaits the homecoming of her suitor-husband with flowers and chocolates, but rather because when the realities of everyday life raise other and more complicated feelings in her, she may think something is wrong with her marriage. The problem lies in a perception of marriage as the culmination of a *passive* passion, something that "happens" to you, that's "bigger than the both of you." A wife who lives by the romantic notion of marriage in her head and ignores the rooted psychological and sociological bases of her mating will not behave in such a way as to encourage the growth of love, something that can surely grow out of passion and with it but needs to be developed in mutual experience. She may begin to feel unloved or bored, not realizing that these feelings arise because she is not actively creative in the working out of decisions and arguments that lead to deepened married love.

The notion of love as passion affects men as well as women, of course, and if it dominates and perseveres without increasing awareness of the need for a more active conception of marriage, it can result in unsatisfying sexual love. We have ample evidence that pleasure in sex requires the active participation of partners who know themselves and can communicate with each other about their most intimate physical and emotional feelings. (The 39 tested fantasies are a desperate device to turn to technology for help where only personal honesty, trust and imagination will work.) A great many older women who were taught that sex was something they shouldn't enjoy or talk about are finding out that mutually pleasurable sex is one of the great sources of human joy and psychological strength. But such sexual relationships do not just happen; they are almost coexistent with our development as human beings. Sex is in the head as well as the body, and when these work together in a relationship aimed at the future, all systems are go. The most profound commentator on human love I have read, the Russian philosopher Vladimir Solovyev, confirms this conjunction in "The Meaning of Love": "Like all that is best in this world, [sex] begins in the dark realm of unconscious processes and relations; the germ and the roots of the tree of life are hidden there, but we must tend its growth by our own conscious action."

Some women try to expel Western culture's deep-rooted romantic illusion in bold new ways. I hear them comparing male centerfolds in the locker room at the tennis courts. Some of my married women students tell me how great it is that women today can seek the excitement they "need" in extra-marital affairs without breaking up the home: any marriage would be dull, they say. All they want is the same freedom as men.

Inevitable as this reaction may be, I believe it keeps women within the same limited sexual sphere of action, now as subject rather than object. But if sex is still the only area of freedom open to women, they are still trapped and unable to exercise full human potentiality.

Yet acceptance and enjoyment of sex are a liberating, transforming attitude when they are not divorced from the full context of human possibility and deeper human commitment. Many young women today seem far healthier in this regard than the women of my day who drank in romantic illusion like ice-cream sodas and waited for their Prince on his white horse. They seem to know that sharing little things in life can be sexually rewarding in the way even arguments were between Tracy and Hepburn. They know they can create an intimate life out of work and even need — buying and cooking nutritious food, clothing themselves in thrift shops — yet these realistic young women are often the ones who hesitate to marry. The Hepburn-Tracy movies might give us a clue here as well. Looking at them now, I see how inevitably, at the end, Spence put Katie back in the kitchen alone, and how she found herself delighted to be there, found it much more fulfilling than being an editor or judge or whatever she had been so brilliantly before. Young people may not have seen these movies, but their parents did. They have experienced the sequel to them in their own homes where real men and women tried to live out their marriages assuming such roles were inevitable. I believe it is the fear that marriage has to involve just such imposed and often hypocritical roles that keeps many young people away from it. Yet this is the second area in which women are complaining most vociferously, against the illusion that "roles" are inherent in the marriage relationship.

In the "Me, Tarzan; you, Jane" world, roles were necessary for survival. In the lived experience of marriage today, couples are forced to choose and shift their roles according to the personalities and the needs of their lives. A given day might call for each partner to deal, separately and competently, with machines, children, various power structures, and an aged aunt who needs a patient ear. Much of the strain on marriage comes when one partner sees the need for flexible responsibilities and the other does not. One attractive mother of three doing a term paper for me that turned out to be a reasoned, personal plea against abortion tells a story I have heard often: as she hands in her paper, late because she had the flu, she confesses how good it is to be divorced. The whole family had been miserably sick, but they had all pulled together in good humor through a week of upset stomachs and schedules. If her ex-husband had been home, she said, he would have kept them in an uproar demanding meals on time and the house in order. His problems — and even hers — may have been psychological or even moral, but similar stories are so frequent they suggest that many marital partners seem unable to adjust early role conceptions to living realities.

Where do such rigid role conceptions come from? They do not exist everywhere. When I asked a national audience of Catholic men and women what they thought about the American tendency to blur usual mothering and fathering roles: sharing the business of nurturing and playing with children, raising, educating, and supporting them, an astonishingly high 86 percent of this highly educated, middle-class audience thought the tendency a healthy one. Evidence suggests that in many ethnic groups and in lower economic strata such roles are so much a part of identity that change is much more difficult.

Such rigid role conceptions have been reinforced historically however by a long tradition in the churches maintaining the existence of a distinct, ready-made loving "feminine nature." Whether or what traits are innately feminine or masculine I would not presume to say: opinion differs sharply here, and we can only decide in this mysterious realm by our own hunches, observations and choice of experts. Yet we do know that the experience of women has been to feel limitation and psychic suffering by assuming passive, unselfish feminine nature as a norm.

This is the third of the "sacred" sexual illusions women challenge today. Just as the experience of marriage negates the viability of passive romance or rigid roles, so do women's experiences negate the usefulness of prescribing "feminine" behavior. It is a commonplace in counseling, for example, that childbearing and rearing induce a loss of identity in the young mother. So much of our identity is socially formed; it is a mutual interaction of the individual, expectations of her and achievement possible to her. The experience of being cut off from the wider community and its values has no doubt been especially difficult for women in this century when the contributions of wives and mothers have been both undervalued and narrowly stereotyped. I saw the results in my mother and in myself, and I continue to see them in my adult women students, who consistently come to class with a much poorer self-image than the promising real persons they are, a gap quite evident to the other students.

This low self-evaluation among many mothers has been aggravated by the geographical isolation of our scattered suburban communities, our lack of natural gathering places and by poor mass transportation. It has often been reinforced, however, by well-meant ecclesial and other expert advice and even praise of "women's nature" as passive and unselfish. Many women who desperately wanted to *be* unselfish finally realized that fitting into this desirable male projection was exactly the wrong way. Only the path of personal independence and self-esteem could lead to unselfishness. Joan Bel

Geddes Ulanov has given us a graphic account of her own evolution from the hopeless attempt to be the perfect Catholic woman, through the breakup of her marriage and consequent depressions to her slow, responsible acceptance of the self she is:

> When religious advisers taught us to hate ourselves, contrary to what Christ said, they set us on a course that could not lead to mature and generous and wholehearted love, because one's attitude toward oneself inevitably colors one's attitude toward others. If you consider yourself worthless this evaluation spills over onto other people. If you consider yourself deserving of stern punishment, you will be apt to apply the same judgment to others. If you distrust yourself it will be hard not to distrust and fear and therefore end by hating others.

Joan survived and lived to tell us how:

> I feel a "peace that passeth understanding," which I used to be told was the sure sign of a good conscience, though I now do many things I once would have considered selfish, even wicked. Having given up the apparently hopeless task of trying to be "good" I find, to my amazement, that I have begun to acquire the patience that eluded me for years. . . . Today I love being me, and wouldn't change places with anyone else in the world ("Charity Really Does Begin at Home — With Oneself," *Holiness and Mental Health,* Paulist Press, 1972).

The grandmother in Tillie Olsen's "Tell Me a Riddle" goes through a similar struggle which serves to unify the many themes I feel converge in this discussion on women and marriage today. Like us, freer to consider the possibilities, this grandmother whose children have grown up and scattered turns down her husband's offer to move to "the Haven" and be treated "like a Queen." "Now I want room," she replies.

> For forty-seven years they had been married. How
> deep back the stubborn, gnarled roots of the quarrel
> reached, no one could say — but only now, when
> tending to the needs of others no longer shackled
> them together, the roots swelled up visible, split the
> earth between them, and the tearing shook even to
> the children, long since grown.

When her daughter asks her why she will not go, she replies:

> "For him it is good. It is not for me. I can no
> longer live between people."
> "You lived all your life *for* people," Vivi
> cried.
> "Not with." Suffering doubly for the unhap-
> piness on her children's faces.

The family discovers she is dying and sends her to visit
each of her children in turn. Yet even as she muses in the
airplane on all her years of motherhood we see that her real
journey is inward:

> Surely that was not all, surely there was more. Still
> the springs, the springs were in her seeking. Some-
> where an older power that beat for life. Some-
> where coherence, transport, meaning. If they
> would but leave her in the air now stilled of clamor,
> in the reconciled solitude, to journey to her self
> (*Tell Me a Riddle,* Dell, 1961).

In this relentless backward and inner journey the grandmother at last awakens in her husband, too, the old, questing
authentic self that enables them to meet again in love and
hope on her deathbed. This fictional American-immigrant
grandmother symbolizes for me what the changed attitudes
of American women can mean to the necessary reshaping of
all our social and interpersonal relationships, among which

marriage is so central. Now, as historically, it is the connection at which personal *becomes* interpersonal, private *becomes* public. A relationship that nurtures the self of both persons involved will turn outward in creative love. As Solovyev insists, "the actual feeling of love is merely a stimulus suggesting to us that we can and must re-create the wholeness of the human being." He goes on to say that the dynamics of such a mutual conjugal love propel it beyond the borders of the home: "Love cannot be realized without a corresponding transformation of the whole external environment: the integration of the individual life necessarily requires the same integration in the domains of social and cosmic life." He sees married love as the best school in which to learn how to defeat egoism, that universal enemy which denies to the selves of others the importance one claims for oneself.

* * *

Many efforts to defend marriage today, under multiple attack from the selfishness encouraged by our culture, tend to falter at this crucial connection. Total Woman, for example, tries to reenergize her marriage by playing sexual games with her husband. Dressing up in cowboy clothes can be fun, but it becomes just another version of mechanical American sex when cut off from the social matrix. Any attempt to "save" marriage that asks the wife to play the role of desired object and to give up her social and intellectual responsibilities undermines the possibility of mature sexual commitment.

Movements like Marriage Encounter that emphasize open, honest communication of feeling between husband and wife can perform an admirable service unless they ask their members to serve "marriage" rather than themselves and the society they live in through the medium of marriage. Trying to defend marriage by isolating it or elevating it into an end in itself is a kind of idolatry. Ultimately it will defeat the ability of marriage to become the sanctuary of personal growth it can be today for those who choose it freely.

Free choice is necessary, commitment that is as open-

eyed as possible. In this atmosphere, marriage is more a risk
than a restriction. It is the one institution that takes the form
its members give it. Time has taught me that form is very
important, far more than empty politeness; it is the inevitable
shaping of anything that exists in the created world. What
is so interesting about marriage is that it is a unique form
created by two persons, a "live" institution that has its comforting passive side.

A young friend, somewhat fearful of restrictions, whose
pregnancy pushed her into marriage, told me recently what a
pleasant surprise it was after years of rather tense living together; the couple found they could work out their responsibilities more easily and joyfully. A formal relationship can
offer the extra support to persons involved so that they can
reach out beyond it. This social consequence of a freely chosen
relationship should remove marriage from the second-class
status it has lately acquired among many ambitious young
women who see it as an easy way out of the obligation to
excel in a career. It is not a way out; to be itself, marriage
does not serve itself. It lives at the juncture of person and
society, enriching both in constant interaction.

Marriage is thus one of the few institutions today that
can strengthen individual human beings to deal constructively
with the impersonal institutions that control so many areas
of their lives. As a freely chosen relationship, it functions
both on the intimate personal level and as a healthy cell of a
larger society of which it is itself a hopeful symbol. Marriages
today are already creating needed new forms. Rosemary
Haughton's communal family, for example, is an attempt to
live married life under conditions that create alternative social
and economic relations even as it answers personal needs for
a supportive group. Voluntary families of many shapes are
now bravely trying to fill the psychological and economic
needs of single people, widows, the divorced, and the just plain
lonely. Such families are indeed heroic.

Clearly even a free and sensible choice will not always
lead to marital success. Some marriages will fail and at their

best there will be much conflict needing resolution. But this is reality, and it must always be accepted if we are to grow. And for its own sake, marriage must insist on the possibility of others *not* to be married. Girls should not feel they have to marry to please their family and society. The right to be single must be equally possible and respectable for men and women if marriage is to be viable.

Nor should the decision to have children be automatic, even in a good marriage, for choice is the burden we must bear if we are to take over the direction of our mechanical culture. I suspect not too many marriages have rested on such choices in the past. Only in this way, however, can marriage be that place where one learns to respect the value of decisions and commitments by others. The children raised in such an atmosphere could be our best hope for a human future.

*   *   *

Looking back, I realize that for a time in my marriage I was swallowed up by my house and that the effects were as sinister as my childish fears had painted them. I began merely *reacting* to the powerful institutions that impinged on my family. Even in dealing with schoolteachers and administrators I too often adopted an emotionally defensive stance — one I believe they fostered, but nevertheless one not in their best interest or mine. Later, when I timorously took a small place "outside" in the local community, I found that the double perspective gave me truer vision as well as enough increase in my sense of self to cope with what I saw. Nagging teachers had their own insecurities; board members and administrators were caught in their own systems and often seemed powerless to change them even when they saw the need to do so.

Able to shift my perspective from that of parent to teacher to citizen to human being, helped by my marriage to do so, I was now in a better position than many in powerful bureaucracies because I did not have the illusion that "they" could solve problems. Learning to trust myself and others, I learned, too, that with people, one could usually dig beneath fears and instinctive rule-following and reach common creative ground.

For me this development was life-giving. That is why I am happy now to work with women going through the same process. Only now, from my experience, do I understand why my mother suffered: she felt the double bind implied in society's expectations of her to be a good wife and mother and the contrary signals that such a role didn't count for much in the "real" world. She could not work out a way then to be herself in ever-widening circles from the home. The ability to be the same person in and out of multiple roles and relationships from private to public is the ability to be fully human. Despite all the decay and chaos of our social environment, this possibility exists today. Even as our image of what men and women are is less clear-cut, the opportunity we offer them to find out is far greater. Marriage can now let us be more ourselves and better able to help one another. I realize now that my father suffered, too. He was rational and disciplined to the extent that he did not feel free enough to indulge the playful, artistic, emotional instincts which were equally his. Today he might have, and might have lived longer.

Henry Adams would be pleased today, too, I think, at what he might see as the emergence of women's instinctive and personal powers into the public sphere whose future he lamented in their absence. He would surely have been pleased to see other men beginning to revalue the "feminine" powers in themselves and in society. My mother would be pleased that women to whom individuals, home and family are of prime importance can feel actively related to the public sphere. Because of these possibilities, I believe marriage today *can* be the most intriguing game in town, one that leads into and out of all the others, enriching them with its homespun force.

4. Personal Views of Marriage: Good Vibrations

Robert Engler

Robert Engler is a refugee to Massachusetts from New Jersey where he was born and spent his first 18 years and most subsequent vacations. He received his B.A. from Notre Dame in 1964, then spent two years as an Extension Lay Volunteer for the Newman Center at the University of Colorado in Boulder.

In 1966 he returned to Notre Dame for an M.A. in theology which he completed in 1968, the same year as his marriage. Taking one year away from academia he worked for the Department of Housing and Urban Development in New York City. He then took up attendance at the Massachusetts Institute of Technology where he ultimately received a master's in city planning.

Presently he is a principal in a Cambridge-based planning and architectural firm, a job which not only brings him great satisfaction but helps to support habits of golf and tennis as well as his wife and two adoring children.

Recent accomplishments include building a dulcimer; a house in Vermont, participation in the births of two children; and living for six years and teaching for two years at a women's college where he was regarded with considerable awe. He is an accomplished cook, excellent at child care, and not bad at wallpapering. Although advancing in years, he still manages to hold his own during lunchtime basketball games with Harvard undergraduates. Bob is currently very much at home on a dead-end street in Newton, Massachusetts.

Dorothea Engler

89

4. Personal Views of Marriage:
Good Vibrations

When asked how I made the decision to marry my wife, I answer "carefully." When asked what is involved in making such a fundamentally important choice, it is more difficult to explain in a way that would be helpful. I can say that I loved her, but that experience is not transferable. O.J. Simpson can say that he moves his legs a certain way and that he carries the football a particular way and tries to look for would-be tacklers, but that isn't very helpful if you're trying to figure out how to run like O.J. After all, I've thought I loved a fair number of young ladies; how did I *know* that Dorothea was *the one?* In retrospect, I would have to say that there were two "keys" to my decision which I trusted.

I trusted those "Good Vibrations" which Brian Wilson wrote about for the Beach Boys about the same time they were happening to us 10 years ago; and I trusted the wise words of the Delphic oracle in ancient Greece (predating Brian Wilson by some years): "Know thyself." Vibrations might also be called intuition, insight or just feelings; they operate on a level of consciousness which is not the normal, everyday, five-senses level. Some people are more attuned to this level than others; I don't feel particularly gifted in this

area, but I was tuned in then — and I trusted those feelings.
I also had an understanding of self which allowed me to trust
in those feelings and vibrations and know that they were real
and true. One's act is never all together, but mine was together enough to know that my love was the commitment-type
variety. This feeling of bravado, however, did not eliminate
the risk. It simply meant that you could live with it — for a
lifetime. This process of getting it all together is not easily
definable; it's a function more of maturity than age. There is
no criterion to indicate you have arrived there. At some point
you simply have to choose.

Dot and I happened to be "there" when we made our
choice, but not without much struggle. We experienced the
strength of our love, but it existed in a realm beyond our
comprehension. While we couldn't figure out our love relationship, we certainly were aware of the daily efforts at working out the relationship which seemed to create so many
obstacles in our path.

> The heart has its reasons which the mind does not
> know. (Pascal)

The external manifestations of our relationship, i.e., the
forms, rather than the experience, consisted of a variety of
standards, expectations, demands and preconceived notions of
what the relationship was *supposed to be* — what good relationships *should be*. I was an expert in living with these
mental pictures of what shape I wanted the relationship to
take. Because I was four years older than Dot, I took for
granted that I had superior wisdom and therefore knew the
changes she had to make in order to get where I thought she
should go. My demands and expectations of her confused my
vision of our relationship as it really was. I continued to love
her despite these barriers I threw in our path.

I was a bearer of "the truth," a keeper of the keys to the
kingdom, a self-appointed apostle to the unbelievers *and* a
male chauvinist. I created and nurtured a teacher-student

relationship with Dot which applied to all phases of her life. Nothing escaped my tutorial eye, including the way she dressed, rode her bike, did her homework, cleaned her apartment or even expressed her own theological views. My overburdening expectations and demands produced constant barriers to overcome in our relationship. Our next two years apart *de facto* smoothed the tensions, as 1,200 miles provided our relationship some welcome physical and psychological space. We managed frequent visits and daily phone calls, but I could no longer monitor everything she did. Given space to breathe, she grew more self-reliant and self-confident. I realized, through my own maturity, that the relationship was growing in proportion to my noninterference with its own dynamic. Getting married brought us back into daily contact and began the process of one household becoming two people.

During those moments when she really told me what I was trying to do to her, and to us, and when I could see that I was programming the relationship rather than experiencing it, I felt genuine pain and consternation. I was thrown "off track," became confused, and, as a consequence, suddenly began to open myself to the insight of what we truly had together, despite what I was trying to do to it.

> God instructs the heart, not by ideas but by pains
> and contradictions. (De Caussade)

The love we shared was, in a real sense, larger than both of us. I couldn't get control of it but could only watch it develop. For someone who had attempted to control everything in his life by anticipating, planning, measuring, evaluating and assigning responsibility, it was significant that this relationship, unlike any previous ones, resisted my efforts. As a result, I felt fear because I wanted to let go and I couldn't. A poem, written during that period, speaks to these feelings.

> She said I love you through the open door
> in a rainy night an I couldn' say nuthin'
> cause I wasn' sure an I'm tryin' hard nowadays

not t' speak when I ain' sure cause I've
been in trouble before f' speakin'
an then regrettin' what I said . . .
But I've been gettin' involved even though
I came back hopin' not t' cause my work
was too important but feelin's in somethin'
I ain' never had much control over an maybe
now's the time t' begin before it's too late
but that ain' f' me t' decide anyhow
an who am I t' stop an start whenever
I damn well feel like it cause that ain' fair
an even worse it stinks of pride . . .
I've been thinkin' an reasonin' an preachin'
but when it comes right down t' it
I don' really know what I'm doin' like always
an maybe I'm sinking or maybe I'm swimmin'
but either way the water could get over my head
an over hers an then we'd be forced t' swim
instead of makin' the choice ourselves . . .
Cause I want t' give her the freedom t' grow
an yet be there t' share in the growth. . .
of both of us an that's hard cause freedom
an sharin' ain' so alike when she's young
an I'm weak an we're goin' too fast
t' catch our breath. . .
But I see somethin' there which is beauty
an I want so bad t' make it grow an be alive
an I want t' make it mine but by grabbin'
f' it I'll destroy it cause right now
it ain' so solid cause it's just been born
an it's got t' be nurtured an I got t' wait
an I ain' so good at waitin' . . .
So I'm askin' f' your help God cause I want
t' be true t' myself an that means the same f' her
an who's t' say anything 'bout that 'cept you
cause I don' know her an I don' even know me
but I'm hopin' t' discover both of us together
if I listen hard enuf t' what you're tryin'
t' tell me which please God I hope I can follow. . .

The love we experienced, however mysterious, and the good vibrations we felt, on whatever level, were strong enough to carry us through the barriers, the battles, and the blind spots to the point of committing our lives to each other. Once having made that decision, marriage became a natural expression of that personal pledge to each other. It was a statement of our intentions to our friends, the Church and the world, and at the same time it was an acknowledgment that we lived in the world as well as in our own minds and hearts. The wedding was that event, agreed upon by society, sanctioned by the Church, and accepted by us, when we publicly and symbolically expressed our bond and our joy. It was, indeed, a peak experience.

Many changes have taken place in our relationship in the past eight years; some are worth noting. In a word or two, the "space" between us has been less cluttered with demands, judgments, and expectations and more open to feel, perceive and experience the other person in each present moment. Our love is stronger and more binding than ever; it is also more freeing so that our relationship flows more naturally. Consequently, it works better. As we work on, first recognizing the little games we play in our lives, such as "being right" and "winning" and "I know it all" and "it's your/his/her/society's fault" (and several hundred variations), and second moving off those games, we are able to see more clearly what is happening now. When you can go with the flow, the relationship takes on a freshness and vitality precisely because it hasn't been planned or programmed (and I am a Planner by trade. . .).

Each morning, if we commit ourselves to finding the truth of every situation, then miracles will come to us all day long. (Sujata)

Giving space to each other is a dominant aspect of our relationship. A phrase commonly used to describe marriage is "making two into one." A more appropriate description of our marriage is the making of two into two. In order to do that, the love in the relationship has to set the other free, not enclose the other in need. This was a problem in our relationship in its earlier days and its earlier years of marriage. It is still being worked out. In observing what comes to mind when I recall those days, I can see how I filled the space in our relationship with my concepts and considerations, and how little I let Dot be who she was. It was a relationship based on needs and demands; it worked well when those needs and demands were met, and it did not work well when they were not.

Standards, norms, comparisons and other aspects of trying to live out the proper forms of marriage, instead of relying on and building on my experience of it, have created barriers to having our relationship work and flow the way it should. Many examples through the course of the past eight years come up such as,

—Wondering if at times I really communicated verbally well enough or often enough with Dot. For example, our friends loved the two-hour drive to our house in Vermont and they could spend the time in conversation, whereas we often had difficulty finding things to discuss. Why didn't we have more to say to each other? Was there something wrong with us?

—Approaching lovemaking at times from a sense of maintaining a "respectable" frequency rate, rather than from a genuine desire to express my love, and wondering if we made love as often as most couples in our stage of marriage.

—Silently blaming Dot when she had trouble losing the weight she gained during her first pregnancy, because she didn't meet my physical standards.

These problems which I manufactured were not solved so much by doing anything differently — that only changes the forms, not the person. They were handled by changing my approach to them, which is no "cop-out" or simplistic solution. It is more radical to transform the person than to change that person's ideas.

Taking responsibility is another vital aspect of getting

our relationship to work. I see taking responsibility as acknowledging that I am the cause in the matter: that is, I create my own situations. This awareness of responsibility for my relationship has meant that I no longer can play the old games of blaming others for things which I felt were wrong or of being the victim of circumstances beyond my control; e.g., "They're doing it to me again," or "society is ripping me off," or "she's making it difficult for me to keep my cool." It was easy to be right and have other people wrong until I realized that game doesn't help our relationship work. I have experienced that I am ultimately responsible for where I am in our relationship.

Keeping agreements is taking responsibility for your actions in the world. For example, I may ask Dot to do something for me, i.e., mail a package, telephone a friend, buy something, and I don't put any time frame on it. Because I expected or assumed that she would do it that day, I might be irritated to learn that she didn't. *I* always do those little chores and favors the same day; *I* even keep my little black book so I don't forget. And Dot should use the same system I do. . . . However, when we make an explicit agreement, which includes the time frame for the action to be carried out, there are no false assumptions or misunderstandings surrounding such a request and the agreement is more often kept. If it is not kept, the person responsible for breaking it acknowledges that, and a new agreement is made. Since we both realize the value of keeping agreements, there is no need to make excuses or blame somebody or something for the broken agreement. "I'm sorry" is fine but secondary to the acceptance of responsibility in the matter; I find that the latter is what allows me and my relationship to work and grow.

Keeping agreements with the children is another aspect of the marriage relationship which I have experienced as having tremendous value. Geoffrey, being almost four, has for some time now been well aware when agreements have been kept by me or not, even when his level of articulateness was not equal to his understanding of the fact that I conned him or didn't take my agreement seriously. I realize now that when I say I will take him to the park on Friday or I will play with him as soon as I finish what I'm doing, I'd better not forget on Friday to take him to the park and I'd better not begin doing something new and put him off because he knows what I'm doing, and it will diminish the value of our relationship.

He understands his agreements about watching television, and picking up toys, for example, and excuses are not part of his act yet. At least he simply states that he is not going to do it — no phony reasons needed. Then he has to take the responsibility for the consequences, e.g., someone may come along and take the toys he left behind.

Reasons for agreements are not as important for personal growth, in my experience, as the agreements themselves. Naturally, some agreements can be viewed as stupid or irrational from other points of view, but the substance of the agreements can be negotiated. Once they are accepted there is a mutual responsibility for keeping them. I can't keep someone else's agreement; it has to become my own in order for me to keep it. If I don't like the agreement, I won't be willing to make it. If I break it, I find that my relationship and my life don't work as well. It's that simple.

The last theme or aspect of making our relationship work is *communication*. Perhaps it is the most important. At any rate, I see love as a function of communication and communication, in turn, as involving all the other themes already discussed: giving each other space, being responsible, and keeping agreements. Communication operates both ways — by sharing your experience with another, and listening so that you *hear* what another is sharing with you.

Communication has taken on new forms for me; rather than communicating to Dot *what* is causing me problems in the relationship, I communicate that I am having a problem with something going on and I just want to share it with her. For example, instead of saying, "Why don't you clean your car; it's really a mess with all the kids' toys left in it," I try to communicate from this point of view: "I have a problem, which I'm working on, about your car being so messy and I'd like to communicate that to you." This form of language appears strange, and it is, because my language (and others' I hear) has been patterned in the former style.

Dot's response to my latter effort can range from a short, "Well, you work it out because messy cars aren't a hang-up of mine" (not a typical reply), to a position of getting what I'm saying and being free to do something about the car or not, as she chooses. She may not feel the car is such a mess, *and* she may clean it simply because of the way in which I brought my concern to her attention. My communication in this form is based on experience and does not impose value judgments on the actions in question; thus, it gives her space to be the cause in the situation rather than being the result of my problems. Once having put out the communication, I can let it go and accept whatever comes up. I don't get stuck with all my considerations and mind games which prevent the growth and movement in our relationship.

Sharing has become easier with the awareness that whatever we are doing is important simply because we are doing it. There need be no other reason. Our actions don't have to be ranked so that only the highest get shared, thus sparing the other from uninteresting commonplace conversation. The realization that *everything* has value is truly uplifting.

Grace is everywhere. (Bernanos)

As our love has freed us to be ourselves and to be more accepting of each other, we have developed a deeper understanding of responsibility in marriage. We are less able to play the old "victim" game (referred to earlier) in which the other is blamed as the cause of one's problem. We both realize that we are each responsible for where we are in the relationship and for what's happening in it. When we have created the situations which makes us uncomfortable, oftentimes it is more efficacious to deal with the cause of the uncomfortable situation — our heads — than with the situation itself. This is not a universal rule; for a hypothetical example: if Dot were beating son Geoffrey into the floor, I don't think I would attempt to deal with that situation by trying to discover why I had a problem with situations in which my son was beaten. However, in many instances, if not all, actions which seemingly have taken on a certain meaning in and of themselves are, in truth, only given such meaning by us. Why we have done so is a more complex issue and usually must be traced back through one's past life. The same action, in fact, can have as many different meanings as are attributed to it by the participants. The act of sexual intercourse — to take an example pertinent to marriage — might be a search for universal wholeness, a gratification of sensual desires, a fulfillment of a need for security, a violation of one's personhood, or an expression of the fulfillment of one's love for the other. It may be engaged in too frequently or not frequently enough, even if the frequency is constant, depending on the partner. The transformation of the actor changes the nature of the action. Jesus said, "What comes out of a man is what defiles a man. For from within, out of the heart of man, come evil thoughts, fornication, theft, murder. . . All these evil things come from within" (Mk 7: 20-23).

The same holds true for all activities in marriage; it's how you approach them that counts. They are as mundane as you believe them to be, or as rewarding as you choose them to be. Our experience of marriage is that the more we choose actions each day to be fulfilling, enriching and exactly what we wanted to happen, the more they are so.

From the outside our marriage may not be soap opera material; it is, however, the way in which we have chosen to share our lives so that nothing is missing and everything is included — joy, reward, purpose, beauty and truth. It's simply — but not so simply — a case of watching our commitment and our love for each other grow and be manifested in thousands of different ways. Who needs pithy words? It works better the more we experience it for what it is — and let it be.

5. Personal Views of Marriage: Pygmalion Speaks

Dorothea Cordova Engler

Dorothea Engler grew up in Colorado in a Cordova/ Valdez clan which included over 80 first cousins. After 21 years in that beautiful state she moved east with her husband to the land of his clan which included one aunt and no cousins. Perhaps as partial compensation, she took up residence in a dormitory at Newton College of the Sacred Heart (now part of Boston College) which also housed 250 students (who might as well have been relatives).

In the past six years she has been a resident director, director of residence life, dean of students and area coordinator. She has dealt with the problems of over 1,000 people — whose names she still remembers. Fortunately, she has participated in their joys as well. As a result, she has developed patience, understanding and compassion — for anyone under 25. During that time she also managed to bring two of her own children into the world and sometimes managed to see her husband when she had no student appointments. She is presently on leave from supporting her husband (financially) after eight years of marriage, and she lives in a relatively quiet house in Newton, Massachusetts. Not yet 30, her next adventure is unknown at this time.

Robert Engler

5. Personal Views of Marriage:
Pygmalion Speaks

Once, during a discussion about marriages, Mom Engler stated that if there had been one thing she knew she could believe in it was the permanence of Bob's and my marriage. "Oh, you'll fight it out," she said, "but I know that your marriage will always survive."

There have been other times of acknowledgment — when friends, students and relatives might tell us they thought our marriage good. I like knowing that others sense a sureness about our marriage; I suppose it means that Bob and I have been able to convey our feelings for each other in such a way that those around us could also get at the truth of our relationship. God knows that there will never be a slow-motion, stop-action, flora-frolicking movie made about Bob and me. That's never been our style. At times strangers might wonder whether Bob and I had ever been formally introduced; but those who know us will affirm our love for each other.

Ours has always been a complex relationship; in discussions with students as to why our relationship works I have been positively unable to set forth any fast principles for a good marriage or relationship. After all, I continue to be

amazed and not amazed, certain and not certain as to why
we chose each other and have been able to live together in
certain grace. I do, though, often speak of three facets of our
relationship which provide some insight into a marriage
which we think works. Those facets are intuition, change,
and responsibility.

*   *   *

How do you know when you tell your story for the 49th
time to the 49th earnest face eager to tell his story for the
53rd time that this could really be *it*? How do you know that
you might finally get beyond the chatty introduction to your
life and into the good parts? Why do you trust yourself to
begin finally to share your life's little secrets? I think it's *intuition* — "the act of knowing without the use of rational processes." I had set out for myself rigid criteria for choosing the
love of my life. It was therefore entirely appropriate for me
ultimately to fall in love with someone who met relatively few
of my standards or expectations, and instead turned out to
be absolutely perfect for me.

True, there were numerous similarities in our back-
grounds and upbringing, but that was also true of others we
had dated. There was, beyond all the reasons for compatibility and all the reasons for incompatibility, an experience
of inspiration (not quite as dramatic as St. Paul's) which led
me to know Bob was the perfect choice.

Accepting the choice was difficult. Formalizing it was
much easier. I'm sure that it was at the point of acceptance
that Bob and I realized our intention to live fully and always
with each other. It then seemed urgent to us that our choice
be acknowledged and blessed by those people and institutions
most important to us. What we hoped to say through our
marriage ritual in a church with family and friends from all
facets and ages of our lives was that Bob and I from all our
past and through all our future were committing ourselves
entirely to each other. For better or for worse we were choosing to work out within the framework of our Church and our
society what we intuitively knew about the other: that each

was perfect and that with love and space and experience we could bring to ourselves and to each other a greater illumination of the truths of ourselves.

Those were the intentions with which we entered marriage. The practical execution was a mite less lofty.

The dynamics of our relationship postwedding paralleled the dynamics of our relationship prewedding with one exception. Whereas I knew that Bob had always taken me seriously, I realized that he now had a stake in my development. That was terrible to contemplate. From the beginning our relationship could best be described as loving adversity. Each of us was quite taken with the other and each of us quite taken with ourselves. There was thus in each of us that desire to comply and please and alternately that equal desire to resist, win, and/or dominate. I think the predominant theme throughout our courtship was Bob trying to dominate and I determined to resist. Bob at this point in his life was working for the Newman Center, caring for the heathens at the secular institution I attended. He was also putting forth a very zealous dogmatism about every facet of the world and life. He was chagrined that I had no strong personal philosophy of the history of mankind and the universe. However, he did see in me a great deal of potential and set forth as sculptor to his Pygmalion.

During the second year of this courtship, Bob had decided that the Newman Center needed a newsletter. Bob's responsibility as editor, publisher, layout artist, etc., was routinely to coerce luckless acquaintances into contributing articles. My assignment was to write about love — the Christian and romantic idea of love. Out of fear of reprisal by the editor I reluctantly accepted. I chose as my theme a line I had read in Teilhard de Chardin: "Love, without the power to change is meaningless." My interpretation at that time was about the necessity for the struggle toward perfection and the urgency to bring not only oneself but others to that struggle. If one were unable to *change* one's habits, character, behavior for the Church, Christ, or a loved one, that love obviously lacked in rigor and sincerity. Real love could make all things possible — make the shy bold, the inattentive ardent, etc. Thus it was necessary to work toward the transformation of one's life and the lives of others. It was not mere coincidence that the editor of the paper was somewhat of the same opinion. I didn't want him totally discouraged.

Bob was rather stern and absolute at this point in his life. But beyond the external subject matter that he was proselytizing, whether at that time it was *Franny and Zooey* or basketball or Christ, the truth that came through in Bob and made him so terribly appealing was his tremendous passion and with that his tremendous caring. I could sense in him a love of the dynamic and because he loved the struggle and the challenges, I knew that he was concerned with growth. At that point in my life, regardless of the form, that was terribly important to me. At times I would be so moved and grateful for his caring that I would vow to change. I would fulfill Bob's expectations. I would become that person that Bob had mysteriously sensed I could be. This desire to change to please Bob, along with a fear of his domination and the loss of my independence, created a lot of tension in the relationship: to be who he wanted me to be/to be who I wanted to be. It never occurred to me to be who I was. So I was locked in struggle both internal and external.

A lot of feelings and experience have gone on finally to bring me to the realization that Bob has always quite clearly known who I was and has always loved me in the same way that I knew who he was and loved him. It is and was totally irrelevant whether or not he was a basketball star or I was a high school queen. There had been for us (and I think there is for all people) a knowing that goes beyond facts — that goes beyond the sequence of events in our lives or our personality profiles.

I used to plague Bob with the question, "Do you love me?" And when he would say yes I would ask again, "I mean, do you *really* love me?" What I wanted him to say was that whoever, whatever I was he unequivocally loved me.

I was too busy asking really to grasp that when he chose me, as when I chose him, we were in fact affirming our unconditional love for each other. Bob has moved off a lot from his expectations for me and I am no longer trying to figure out what kind of person he wants me to be and how I am measuring up. I know now that Bob and I indeed knew each other when we decided to get married. It just took us a while to discover what we knew. It has only been recently after years of marriage that instead of asking I have been able to say to Bob, "I know you love me." And Bob says, "That's good."

Today I can read the same words from de Chardin and find quite different meaning. They say more to me now about allowing and encouraging the dynamic in others, about love which does not impose limits but allows space and encourages development — truly the freeing kind of love. Out of this love comes change. The power of this love derives not from tension and force but from openness.

I feel infinitely freer today to be my own person than I have ever felt before and that is due to the changes not in Bob but in my attitudes toward myself which then allowed for the changes to take place with Bob. For some time I felt that my acceptance could be complete only through Bob's acceptance of me. It is clear to me now that acceptance can only be accomplished through my own peace with myself. It is clear to me that in our relationship, bound by the agreements we made in marriage, it is all right with Bob for me to be and do what I want. And I don't mean all right in a patronizing way, because the practical acceptance of my choices is at times as difficult for Bob to actualize as it is for me. I have also found that I must take total responsibility for my choices, my positions and my role.

I think one of the most important realizations in my life and in my marriage was the recognition that I was not a victim of relationships, circumstances, or of the happenstance of my sex. The experience of watching and living with my own mother in her various roles as wife, mother, teacher, participant in Church, politics and community projects was fundamental in forming my impressions that a woman in marriage could be multipurpose and find fulfillment in all those aspects of her life. The women's liberation movement was helpful in promoting the social and political climate which made it practical and respectable for women to play any number of roles either simultaneously or sequentially in life. I must, however, disagree with those factions of the women's movement which find it necessary to designate men as the victimizers and women as the victims. I bought that point of view for some time and it worked well. I could blame failure, frustration, misunderstanding, nonfulfillment on a culture which suppressed women. On a more personal level, I could blame Bob for any part of my life that seemed to be withering. I don't accept myself as victim any longer. I know now that I used that game as an excuse rather than face up to the reality of my *responsibilities*. What "liberated" me was not a change in others' attitudes toward me but a change in my attitudes about myself.

Where once I held Bob responsible for my boredom or loneliness, for creating new directions in his life which seemed to end satisfying situations in mine, for going off to play golf while I stayed with the baby, I can't see that as valid anymore. I wasted a lot of time and clouded up a lot of issues — some trivial, some important — because I failed to formulate solutions that were possible, and principally because I failed to express the way I really felt about many things that came up in our lives. My old method of operation was to save up my complaints for some explosive situation when I could bring them out and completely sandbag Bob with a moundful of resentment and hurt and anger that would really upset him. I won a lot of arguments that way and that was my racket — silent suffering and then smashing righteousness.

As I told Bob recently, arguing isn't as much fun anymore because we've stopped trying to make either one of us right or wrong. What we try to do now is to understand the situation which makes the necessity for right-wrong stuff irrelevant to solutions. Bob and I share our thoughts as they

come up, our anger when it comes up, our dissatisfaction
when it comes up. There is rarely time for any wound to
fester. There are very few opportunities for me to sit around
and feel sorry for myself and there is no question that I
now see more clearly my own foibles and shortcomings. Every
situation is now an opportunity not to work on the other person but to work on oneself. Accepting the responsibility oneself and removing the blame from those around one certainly
creates the opportunity to see the other person more clearly
and to eliminate the character assassination that it is often
such a pleasure to do. Life is much cleaner, simpler, and much
more real when one deals with the reality of the present.

I've discovered that my life works better and my relationships work better if I communicate honestly instead of
biting the bullet. Problems clear up; they don't always disappear, but at least they aren't clouded over with complicated
and mucky emotion and misconception.

Bob and I find we are happier. I find I am able to be
happy as a working woman when I am working and have
even begun to allow myself to be happy as a mother and
housewife — something I had previously thought of as an
"and-what-else-do-you-do?" occupation. I am happier because I know that in every moment of my life I can choose
to do what I am doing. Bob and I take each other more
seriously in that our commitments and obligations to each
other are as much to be met as those we make to other people.
Familiarity is no excuse. We extend this same seriousness to
our children and feel that if they can believe our word at age
two they will believe it at nine and 13 and 20. We have
experienced that the real person in a child is not a future idea
but a very present one and that it is important at all times
to treat two-year-olds and 40-year-olds with the same integrity and courtesy. It is only the subject matter that varies
with age. The level of commitment should be the same.

So there is a certain amount of amazement with which
I reflect upon our marriage and note that it has indeed been
the gentler sides of our relationship that have dominated

(both in intensity and duration). It is no small wonder to me
that humor, kindness, helpfulness, sensitivity, expansiveness,
spirit, generosity, time and patience have truly bound our
marriage. And I acknowledge the anger, the hurt, the selfishness, stubbornness and loneliness which have also been a part
of our marriage, for they also are great indicators of who we
are and what we are about. The times of passion, the
moments of great and deep sharing, the times of growth and
insight have found us in both dark and light moments. The
twists of life surprise us at the best and worst possible times.

It is surprise which urges us to live in the present. For
we have found that past and future cloud one's perception
of the amazing present and limit the possibilities of life. We
are not living together for the rest of our lives but instead try
to be together every day. That's how it comes. Bob and I
have been the best of friends and the best of lovers. It is to
me a great happiness to know that the ache that has been in
me to be myself and to show myself to another in all my big-
ness and littleness has begun to be realized.

I always used to marvel when I would see old couples
married for scores of years absorbed in conversation with each
other. I used to wonder what they could possibly be discussing
after all those years. Hadn't it all been said? I suppose I
have just begun to realize that the more shared the more
opened. And so the endless possibilities always to be deeper
friends and closer lovers.

6. To Be Better Than We Are Wont

Richard Conklin

Dick Conklin is a man of many parts — a perceptive, complicated, faithful spouse. His ironic manner masks a sensitive and nostalgic nature. He admits his mistakes, encourages independent growth, ventures solutions for everyone's complaints, and keeps the house in good repair.

His career began at De LaSalle High School in Minneapolis, writing class skits and editing the paper and yearbook. He went on to the College of St. Thomas in St. Paul, and will be long remembered for his column in the student newspaper in which he frequently attacked and satirized a neighboring college and my alma mater, the College of St. Catherine.

Our paths crossed briefly, but it was only after Dick had served as a reporter on the St. Louis Post Dispatch *and the* Minneapolis Star *that we courted and married. He was director of the news bureau at St. Thomas and taught journalism there until he came to Notre Dame in 1967.*

I could certainly have married a less private person, but would have missed the challenge of discovering this man. I enjoy both the stimulation of his perceptive mind and his uncritical acceptance of those nearest to him, even when sorely badgered. He's a good man to have on one's side.

Annette Conklin

115

6. To Be Better Than We Are Wont

Young Catholics nowadays get married in a variety of ways. Some still visit the rectory to clear the music with their pastor, while others do their own thing with Bob Dylan lyrics and self-composed vows recited on an island in Lake Michigan, on a day — one hopes — when it does not rain. Yet, they all have one thing in common. Those getting married usually do not know what they are doing. In fact, one of the ironies of the Catholic marriage ceremony is that the only people present who know what marriage is all about have no lines to speak. In the Roman Church, the chief witness, shrewd and discerning though he may be, has only a second-hand knowledge of marriage. The couple getting married know even less. As one observer put it, they "expect marriage to be a combination of a religious conversion experience, a successful psychoanalysis, and a vacation in a tropical paradise." The only participants who have some practical wisdom regarding what the couple are getting into are those who have lived a marriage — those parents out there in the congregation who indulge each generation's inclination to think it has invented marriage, and who stand mute and pray.

117

What are the thoughts of married people witnessing a marriage in that church in Beloit (or on that sunny island in Lake Michigan)? To listen to vows and know their awesomeness is to renew one's own (and realize their awesomeness anew). It is also to ponder a curious genealogy — how everyone participating in that sacramental event is there because of someone else's promise. We are each a link in a long chain of commitments we did not forge, and we gather at a marriage to see a part of this continuum at a moment when it appears most discrete. We can but dimly know the joys and anguish, the laughter and despair which over time formed us, but we do sense that it begins with the kind of commitment Christian marriage asks one person to give another.

This commitment is like no other, because it is open-ended. That is why those who get married know not what they do, know not where the relationship will lead. And that is why no preparation is adequate to the demands marriage imposes, even as family, church and society are constrained to try. One is tempted to offer the advice medieval cartographers put at the edge of their flat world: "Out there are dragons."

Yet marriage will likely outlive its current bad press. The Roper Organization recently surveyed a national sample of men and women (it is not without significance that it was commissioned by the Virginia Slims cigarette company) and found nine of 10 young persons believing in marriage, albeit a shared one in which household chores and child-rearing are mutual responsibilities. The continuing popularity of marriage is indicated most dramatically in divorce statistics. While one in three marriages is now statistically doomed to founder in this country, the U.S. Census Bureau tells us that three-fourths of all divorced men and two-thirds of all divorced women remarry, usually within five years after separation. One in four marriages is the second, third or fourth for one of the partners, revealing, perhaps, both the persistence of hope and the doggedness of immaturity, as well as the cultural acceptance of serial — but not contemporaneous — plural marriage. Divorce repeaters also obscure the marital picture, overshadowing the true number of persons still living with their first spouse. For example, a recent survey of University of Notre Dame alumni revealed continued stability of marriages, the average divorce rate being only 5.6 percent.

These statistics noted, marriage is ever a risk. One can no more guarantee those at the altar happiness than dispense them from hurt. Marriage can force personal growth that could not be fostered in any other way, and it can also unfold as enervating disappointment. It may reap a reward as unconditioned as its vow, and it might quietly — and for reasons no one is quite sure of — fail. For some, marriage will be a graced experience. For others, it will entwine pain and bitterness. For all it will be hard work.

Hard work is not an easily accepted metaphor for marriage. It seems bleak, but it cuts between the inexperienced naivete of some and the facile cynicism of others to draw a working picture of the way commitment is reflected in the day-to-day transactions of marriage. Marriage *is* difficult, and it *does* require exertion. "Hard work" may not be a pleasant figure of speech, but it is an accurate one.

If an open-ended commitment is at the heart of the marriages we call Christian, and if marital unions grow or atrophy to the extent spouses are willing to work at the often-ragged edges of their relationship, we have a useful way of looking at other notions of the way men and women ought to live together, many of them admittedly more popular than ours.

For example, among the more ludicrous approaches to marriage which accompanied the early days of the women's liberation movement was the idea of marital contracts. The couple sits down and draws up an agreement — who is going to take out the garbage on alternate Tuesdays and who is going to have what Saturday afternoons free for "cultural experiences." If ever a marriage is doomed at the start, it is one in which the couple thinks it can encompass its demands in fine print, affix signatures, and live on in notarized bliss.

The commitment is not a legal piece of paper. It is important to remember this because the "legal restrictions" of marriage are so often referred to as the reasons why persons avoid it. The reality of marriage is quite the opposite — law binds little; promise, a lot. Law demands of us the minimum; love coaxes us beyond that. Renegotiation of the marriage covenant — like the original agreement — hinges ultimately on such things as trust, respect, understanding, and compassion — and the law can enjoin none of these.

The personalist philosophy of marriage, which permeates much current literature, has a notion as wrongheaded about marriage as that of the legalists. It is what I call the *laissez-faire* approach, in which each partner is encouraged to seek his or her own greatest good, and out of this is supposed to come something called a "mature relationship." It's a great theory; the only thing wrong with it is that it does not work. The marriage relationship is worked out at close quarters. There are too many things which rankle, too many points of rasp, too many collision courses. Marriages work only if both partners are occasionally willing to defer their own best interest to another's, to back up when the enticement is to move forward for "self-realization," to sacrifice when the opportunity is present to aggrandize. I sometimes think that when Christ asked us to "lay down our lives for our friends" he had in mind not a violent death but a more muted form of self-effacing love. The problem is one of fashioning, not independence, but interdependence — and that is a much more challenging task.

Any contemporary discussion of marriage in light of commitment has to deal with cohabitation outside of marriage, a subject on which I have applied for the status of conscientious objector.

The first form, casual cohabitation, is the easiest to discuss. Even the sociologists, who have not been the most perceptive observers of the contemporary man-woman scene, seem to agree that the "sexual liberation" which freed sex from relationship has run its course, leaving in its wake men and women shunned because they resisted peer group pressure to trivialize sex and men and women victimized because they purchased it oversold. Too many social scientists had talked about "sexual liberation" with all the superficiality of Hugh Hefner. They were countered by theologians who made of sex an abstraction carrying so much symbolism it boggled the experience. Only recently have we managed to improve the conversation about sex by sending engaged people to talk, not with sociologists or theologians, but with married couples, and by adding married lay persons to those counseling young Christians on sexual relationship.

If there is any one thing experienced Christians ought to tell less experienced Christians about sex, it is that it is not where the action is in marriage. Most sexologists will dispute that; they are inclined to see all marriage problems as bedrock. On the other hand, marriage counselors, if I read them rightly, say the opposite — people who come in with "sex problems" turn out to have marriage problems. I'm inclined to agree with the counselors. This is not to deny that there are sexually dysfunctional people who are helped by the research and treatment of legitimate scientists like Masters and Johnson. It is only to point out that taking this group as a guide to how sex looms in a normal marriage is like taking people in psychoanalysis as typical of psychological stability.

We pander to the young when we accept at face value their own overemphasis on sex. Let them read the gymnastics manuals (sexual curiosity outlasts any culture's sex education), but remind them that the psychosocial intricacies of the love relationship in marriage are not solved by mechanistic sexual proficiency. "My fiancé and I have discussed our attitude toward oral sex," one student proudly informed me. "Fine," I replied, "but I think your time would be better spent figuring out how you are going to fit two careers into one marriage." Our culture is inclined to talk about sex as though it existed apart from relationship. We have to keep reminding young persons that the quality of the whole relationship is what demands continued scrutiny, especially be-

cause of the temptation to exploit sexually other persons and
delude oneself in the process.

As one insightful marriage counselor put it, "The Play-
boy-hedonistic philosophy that 'anything is all right as long
as nobody is hurt,' cannot compete with the Judeo-Christian
tradition that 'nothing is right unless somebody is helped.' "
The argument, for example, that premarital intercourse will
help one learn something about marriage is unconvincing. It
more often offers instruction in sexual technique than en-
lightenment about sexual intimacy.

Trial marriage — in which cohabitation is equated with
courtship — is a second variation. The problem here is that
there is no such thing — there is no true marriage unless there
is unreserved commitment, and where there is a "trial" there
is conditioned commitment.

It is also misleading to endorse, as many do, cohabitation
as a preparation for marriage. Touted as an alternative to
the discredited role-playing of the dating game, it falls short
of coming to terms with the necessity of full commitment.
It holds back, avoiding the vulnerability upon which together-
ness is built. And it is not critical enough about sex, too often
giving it center stage by default. Psychologically, trial marriage exponents, while they talk a game of realism and prag-
matism, are actually the last of marriage romantics. They live
on the hope that someday the violins will swell and the uncertainty about loving another human being will be resolved.
They await the very understanding they have to earn by risk-
ing marriage in the first place. Insight does not precede commitment; it grows painstakingly out of it.

The third variant of cohabitation is one in which the
participants view it as an alternative to marriage. My half-
brother is one of these. He has lived longer with one woman
outside the bond of matrimony than many more formally
constituted unions have lasted. He is most certainly not involved in a casual relationship, and he objects strenuously to
being considered pursuing a trial marriage. He insists that
his life-style has its own integrity, ready to be judged alongside
that of marriage.

If the very guts of marriage are not found in its legal trappings, why gainsay those who are sincerely working at a relationship without them? But if the honest commitment is there, what prevents those who have made it from declaring it publicly, and inviting support from others embarked on the same precarious journey? I cannot but believe the principal appeal of cohabitation, even at this level, is still that it is comparatively impermanent. As much as my half-brother would object to the term, it is a halfway house, a place in which mature decision can be delayed. It remains, for example, a situation in which the root question of children nags but does not confront.

The question of children is important because it is imbedded in the larger issue of growing up by growing into (not away from) responsibilities. Children mark a real difference. The relationship now widens, the focus shifts, the vulnerability increases, the delights intensify. Parenting presents a new set of choices. One can ignore one's children at their peril, or try to live through them at one's own peril. Children intrude upon a carefully built up man-woman relationship, challenging its latent potential for selfishness while deepening its staying power.

The planning latitude that contraception has allowed today's young married is a mixed blessing. It means that children will have a more deliberate reception, but, Planned Parenthood's assumptions aside, it does not guarantee an extended welcome. The other side of birth control is not much discussed. What of those young married people who first postpone children in circumstances in which their own parents had them by comparative happenchance and then seem to drift into a childlessness less and less defensible? A priest once told me of being in an extremely well-appointed suburban home of an obviously affluent young couple who told him they were reluctant to bring children into a world "fraught with misery." If such skittishness had been evident through history, few children would have been brought into the world, which is normally in a mess. It is no plea to return

to a *status quo ante* in terms of contraception to argue that
the freedom of choice it offers can be well-used or ill-used.

Some marriages begun with the best of intentions fail,
as did that of my mother and father. But the only thing in
the end which makes marriage work is, to repeat, the ability
to risk the very vulnerability which makes its failure so costly.
There is no way around it. Cavils about the legalism of marriage are just that. When cohabitation relationships founder,
their appeal, curiously enough, is to the very rule of law whose
role in human affairs they have scorned. (In St. Paul,
Minnesota, nonmarried couples come to conciliation court
to settle claims to property accumulated during cohabitation.
They do it without cost of counsel, and it is called the "four-
dollar divorce" in reference to the minimal court fee.)

There is no rejoicing in any parting, whether or not
accompanied by attorney fees. Lately my wife and I have
watched marriages of too many friends end, standing as close
as beckoned, feeling helpless, trying not to judge, and being
kept from disdain by seeing in failed marriages the very
problems with which we struggle daily. There is no relationship on earth that is, at one and the same time, so deep and
so fragile as marriage. If Christian marriages do, indeed, die,
what say we about permanence? We keep it as an ideal, and
we make it as easy as possible for those whose marriages end
to make new beginnings.

I leave it to the experts to do theology on this issue, but
I warn them away from one tempting path — the search for
the so-called "innocent party." There may be a few clear-cut
cases — such as outright abandonment — but in most failed
marriages there is no "innocent party." I once had a theory
that marriages broke up when there was an uneven level of
maturation between partners. My wife argued that this was
only another simplistic analysis, unable in the end to account
for the complexity of the human behavior involved and serving only to allow me sneakily to place blame. She was right.
In order to handle compassionately the thousands of Catholics
who find themselves in failed marriages, we need some sort

of theological amnesty — not a doomed attempt to ascribe guilt but a willingness to forget the sins of both parties. And we need to do this in such a way as not to weaken the claim of permanence because it, as part of the open-endedness of the marriage commitment, can challenge us to be better than we are wont.

To be better than we are wont . . . that phrase is worth repeating, for on it turns the whole rationale for marriage as Christians are called to live it. If two people can create mutual space wherein they can share pain and joy, forgiveness and understanding, they will also grow up . . . in His grace.

7. Marriage: An Old, New Fairy Tale
Rosemary Haughton

It is, I feel, almost an impertinence for me to "introduce"
Rosemary Haughton: so often I am introduced to people as
"Rosemary's husband" or even as "Mr. Rosemary Haugh-
ton"! Nevertheless the editor has asked that I do so, so here
goes.

Rosemary is the woman I married in 1948, the woman
I took "for better, for worse," before God and our friends and
relations in Westminster Cathedral's Lady Chapel. At least,
she is that woman and at the same time she isn't. So much
that was invisible in her then has since come so prominently
into view (my view — I'll ignore the public view here). The
girl I married was retiring, even shy, in company, and organ-
izing housework was a burden of considerable mystery and
complexity. She wanted a large family but the first baby's
arrival was a difficult, painful and even perhaps a traumatic
experience for her (and indirectly for me). She was an en-
thusiastic and gifted artist but had never written anything
much more than dozens of long fluent letters to me during
our courtship. Her schooling had been spasmodic and she
had never passed or even taken a public examination.

Yet now she has borne me 10 children — and if that phrase offends as smacking of "male chauvinism," I would reply that it says no more than the literal truth: she has carried them (two at once on two occasions) for and from me. She has brought them up — even educating some at home for a period — through innumerable difficulties. She is easy in company (though she'll never be good at "small talk"). She organizes the household like a whirlwind. She has written more books, not to mention articles and essays, than I can count (I keep on coming across one I didn't even know about!). She lectures frequently, thereby contributing very largely to the maintenance of the "household" of 20 that we now consist of. She has taken part in radio programs and appeared on television and has now received two honorary doctorates.

So Rosemary is not the woman I married in 1948. (Nor, of course, am I the man she married.) She is the woman whom that girl has become partly, at any rate, through her having then taken me "for better, for worse," but partly also because she has accepted the "give and hazard all" aspect of the marriage hero that she refers to in this essay. There is much of Rosemary that I still don't know; I continue to learn (often from what she writes), as is the case in all human relationships.

Though I don't always agree with, or even understand, all Rosemary writes, what she writes here makes profound good sense to me. It may be argued that it is a theory, but it is a theory that we are at present attempting to put into practice in the Lothlorien community of which about half are members of our family and their children. And so far it seems to be working, though exactly what it will eventually become none of us, I think, feels competent to prophesy.

Algy Haughton

7. Marriage: An Old, New Fairy Tale

The coming together of two people in marriage is a new beginning. From the old, a new life emerges, a life for two, but in its two-ness expressing a wholeness whose limits are out of sight.

This new beginning can be the beginning of a quest, not just for married happiness but for life for the whole people. What I am suggesting is that we need, now, to think of marriage as a "hero role," undertaking a hard but vital quest, a mission on which the future of many people depends.

This idea is embedded in Jewish and Christian story. The people of Israel is a family affair, whose myth of origin involved a married couple called to enact this hero role. They were pioneers in a new venture whose significance they barely understood and often doubted. But the faith that drove Abraham and Sarah, with whatever hesitations, to undertake a totally new kind of life, was "reckoned unto him for righteousness." It worked because as an enterprise it made good sense, even if its beginnings looked extremely precarious and risky. Abraham and Sarah were not, in the story, very heroic characters by nature. Abraham is shown as timid and inclined to hedge his bets, and capable of brutality; Sarah is

131

cynical and tough-minded. But for that very reason they are
an excellent symbol of marriage-as-hero. The symbolic hero
emerged from their response to the demand made on them.
The hero always must emerge in response to a real and definite need, as shown by circumstances. But not all do, in fact,
respond. Certainly marriage has not normally seemed an
obvious "hero evoking" situation. And in order to understand why I think we need to realize the inherent "hero role"
in marriage, and why that is a task for Christians especially,
it is necessary to see why, until recently, it was difficult to
think of it in that way.

Human life is shaped by myth — that is, symbolic patterns by which (even without knowing it) we interpret our
experience of living and give it meaning. One of the dangers
of our time is that our culture has failed to realize this. Whenever people refuse to recognize the power and function of
myth it still works (that is how we are made) but it works in
ways we don't realize, and can be destructive.

These myths are expressed in stories, sometimes "fairy
tales," sometimes legends about real people who come to
"embody" the myth in a typical form. For instance, the
courage and resourcefulness and almost superhuman abilities
of the pioneer making a New World are embodied, for many,
in such a character as Davy Crockett, whose historical career
is selectively used, embroidered and added to, to provide the
right kind of hero. The need for heroes creates them, in every
age, but the pattern is the same as that of the fairy-tale hero,
the often neglected poor boy or youngest son who is sent on
a quest, when his "betters" have failed. His mission is to save
the people — from dragons, or enemies — or to heal the
sick king (who *means* the *people*) by fetching the water of
life, or the bird of happiness. The meaning is always the same.

This is the hero myth, but there is another myth which
has shaped Western experience for hundreds of years, and
that is the romantic myth. And this is the only one we have
really been willing to recognize, and have therefore overdone
it. The romantic myth first arose in about the 12th century,

and the archetypal form of it is the story of Tristan and
Isolde, the lovers driven together by a passion they could
neither explain nor control, seeking each other in spite of
every law, loyalty or interference, and finally dying in each
other's arms, since such passion can only find its fruition in
death. Symbolically, it expresses the intense and extraordi-
nary effect of love, opening up the depth of personality,
destroying all lesser emotions, which is an essential part of
spiritual growth. It was a protest against loveless political
and mercenary marriage, and all systems that violate human
feelings.

When, by the end of the 18th century, marriage had
become devalued by overmuch emphasis on the respectability
it bestowed and the virtues it encouraged, as well as — medieval fashion — the inheritances it secured, a great new explo-
sion of the romantic myth offered a way of discovering a
profound personal and spiritual meaning in the transaction
itself, as well as in "illicit" passion on the medieval model.

In course of time, the romantic myth was encouraged
(though not recognized *as* a myth) and indeed blown up out
of all proportion to other aspects of human life, just because
so much of the rest of life was deprived of meaning. Being
in love is a *real* experience, one with profound consequences,
and deep roots in the unconscious mind. It essentially presents
a picture of total, single-minded, world-rejecting passion; it
is a potent and important symbol: the coming together of
earth and heaven, the death and new birth, the divine
marriage.

But it becomes misleading and dangerous if men and
women imaginatively identify themselves with the archetypal
lovers. Few are capable of fulfilling such a role as a career,
and in trying to be fantasy Tristans and Isoldes many fail to
make use of the symbols in the proper way, to help them
develop aspects of themselves. Instead, they live fantasy lives,
and that is what the romantic myth, taken out of ritual
and symbolic context and translated into a way of life, has
encouraged people to do.

By now, the contradictions implicit in this have become too apparent, too destructive, and also too ridiculous, to be allowed to continue unchallenged. The myth is a good myth, but, thank God, the Romantic Era is over. The great romantic symbols are sad, discredited ghosts, gibbering faintly in little magazines.

*   *   *

It was a luxury, anyway, a way of thinking about marriage and love and sex which only could flourish among people whose lives were secure and comfortable enough for them to have time to examine the quality of their feelings and make value judgments about them. For when you are poor life is a struggle of a basic kind, a struggle for money, for food and rent, a struggle against dirt and fatigue, and ill-health and loss of hope. In this kind of life you may marry because you fall in love, but thereafter it counts as a good marriage if the husband earns enough to live on, is honest, reasonably faithful, doesn't hit his wife or children, and is not drunk more than occasionally. It is a failure if he is lazy and shiftless, or violent, a heavy drinker or a criminal, or just walks out and disappears. It is a success if the wife is reasonably good at cooking and cleaning, faithful (most of the time), fond of the children and not easily irritated. It is a failure if she neglects the children grossly, is unfaithful or spendthrift or a disastrously bad housekeeper. And even when many of such unpleasant kinds of behavior exist, it is surprising how marriages hold together, for no reason anyone can see, except inability to discover or imagine an alternative. Great heroism can grow out of such difficult lives, but there is not much room for romance, and preoccupation with the finer points of relationship belongs to a different world. "Marriage enrichment programs" simply don't come into the picture. Anxiety about not being "fulfilled" is a luxury for the comparatively prosperous and leisured.

It is true that the insights developed by people concerned for the quality of married love, inspired unconsciously by the real power of the romantic myth, have enormously enhanced understanding of what such a relationship can be, and what it can do for human growth toward maturity. They have helped Christians to realize the "charity" of married love. But the weakness of the emphasis on arriving at a high quality of married life (much needed though it was) was that it tied in too easily with the romantic premise that quality of feeling not only brings about, but *justifies* a union, married or not, and that therefore inadequacy of feeling, lack of "fulfilment" or indeed any kind of emotional hardship indicate that the union is no longer justified and can and should be dissolved, by law if that is necessary. Those who, for the sake of the children or out of religious conviction, continue with what the romantic ideal labels as an emotionally substandard relationship are therefore convinced that they are among the failures, and must live an "empty" relationship, even though, by other standards, their lives are reasonably contented and creative. This is a demoralizing and debilitating feeling to have, and a great waste of human potential, for the romantic doctrine does not allow of a second chance. It is a once-for-all, consuming experience and an implicitly elitist doctrine, a teaching for the few who are capable of great passion. This romantic judgment has found its way into Christian thinking about the nature of marriage. From an extreme of judging the validity of marriage by purely legal and physical criteria, which does at least give every marriage a chance, it has moved to another extreme, that of judging by purely emotional ones, which automatically excludes all whom background, temperament or circumstances have rendered emotionally uneducated or handicapped.

But human realities can be reduced neither to the physically provable (whether by completed intercourse or a properly attested document) nor to what can be related to the myth of transforming passion.

Human life, and therefore marriage, is made up of a vast variety of feelings and acts and thoughts and relationships, and we need myth to give them shape. The Romantic

myth is beautiful, but inadequate, and its importance has
depended largely on the general feeling of lack of any but
private relevance in domesticity in our culture. If the domestic
is the *only* area you can really shape, then a myth which
makes sense of that is obviously vital to self-respect and hope.
"Private life" is, by definition, something aside from the big
issues, the ones that make history, and that is where we have
put marriage. We in the West accepted that separation,
accepted the irrelevance of marriage as a public fact, and
lived marriage as a kind of backyard set apart for private
emotional cultivation, using a romantic yardstick to measure
our success, even as Christians.

My thesis is that this was a disastrous mistake, and although we cannot undo the past, we can take hold on the
present in order to make the future. That is why we need to
recognize a different myth, that of the hero, and to perceive
that the hero is not necessarily a "great leader," perhaps of a
revolution, but simply one who realizes the human calling,
which is to go out and discover the future, symbolically to
find the water of life, rescue the princess and kill the dragon.

At different times, to be sure, different classes of people
have evoked the hero symbol and expressed its meaning in
their lives, and inspired others to develop the inner hero in
themselves. At one time it was explorers, at another pioneers
in covered wagons, at another scientists, at another nationalist
leaders. Now, it is the turn of married couples, strange as that
may sound to our romantic ears.

Consider the situation. We live in a society in which the
inherited framework of daily life is still more or less (usually
less) functional but where it is losing credibility and therefore
effectiveness, as it increases in complexity and cost, and goes
gradually out of control. To mention only a few areas, the
traffic in big cities is a problem already far beyond solution;
schooling seems less and less about education and more and
more of a self-justifying bureaucratic process enforced by law
and leading too often to jobs no sane person would want if
they weren't paid for them; health care increases in cost and

decreases in effectiveness, so that those who most need it are least likely to get it; "welfare" is becoming a huge sick joke; even the most dedicated social workers often live on the edge of cynical despair; religious organization holds churches together administratively but the vital religious things tend to go on somewhere else (though to do them justice, the churches are far more aware of this problem, and prepared to tackle their "irrelevance" than any government structures). One could go on. Prisons, postal services, government itself — all become less and less relevant to what any actual people actually need, and actively oppressive in relation to some "underdeveloped" economies. Ivan Illich diagnosed the illness, and many others have done so since, and suggested all kinds of remedies, the most convincing prognosis being that the whole thing will collapse under its own weight, and that the best hope is to wait and make plans to rebuild among the ruins.

However, while waiting, people have to live. What we need is a strategy which embraces the depressing interim of gradual (or possibly war-accelerated) dissolution, but provides some kind of starting point for reconstruction. (Cultures, even ours, change slowly and bit by bit, except in wartime.) This is what the hero is needed for, now, and this is why married couples are the ideal people to embody the kind of hero required.

* * *

I referred earlier to Abraham and Sarah, a couple who embodied the hero myth, going out in obedience to make a new future, with only their willingness and the power of the Lord who sends them (in the fairy tales usually a king) to see them through. The idea runs through the New Testament, too. Jesus is so clearly a hero figure that it used to be fashionable to suggest that was all he was — just another divinely inspired Man with a Mission, destined to be rejected, killed and subsequently worshiped. The gospel call to "leave all things" to "seek the Kingdom," the treasure, the elusive fish, is a clear (and no doubt intentional) reminder of tales and myths about seeking for Life, and Truth, in unlikely ways and places. Clearly, also, heroism is needed to do it. The demand is inescapable. To follow Christ the hero is to enter into a hero role also. But it cannot be done in pride of achievement, as all the tales of older, clever sons who failed on the quest remind us. Humility — that is, realism — is essential.

Jesus didn't say much, directly, about marriage, and what he said was mostly negative. He even suggested that some people had to do without it if they were to follow the hero calling. But he said a great deal about selfless love, and about courage. This is important, because in our efforts to sort out the distinctive character of marriage as a Christian way of life we have sometimes lost sight of a major theological fact about Christian marriage: we are Christians first, then married Christians. It is because all Christians are called that married Christians are called. All are redeemed, forgiven, sent. The specialness of marriage for Christians makes sense only on this foundation. It is not that married people have a special kind of Christianity, but that Christians have a special kind of marriage, and St. Paul most clearly shows what is special about it.

Paul was not very interested in marriage, and seems to have discussed it only when called on to settle practical problems, though the traditional Jewish bridal motif, the marriage of Yahweh and Israel, was clearly in his mind as a justification and context for Christians wanting to marry. But, paradoxically, it is what he doesn't say about marriage which is most illuminating, for his scant and even rather impatient references are always set in a wider context, one which he does treat at length. When discussing whether young widows should marry again, he feels (in view of the impending end of all things) that such a widow would do better to stay single, but he says she is certainly quite free to marry, only it must be "in the Lord." One obvious sense of this phrase is that she should marry only a Christian, but Paul normally uses the word "brother" to refer to a fellow Christian. The phrase "in the Lord," however, he uses many times in other contexts. He greets people "in the Lord," wants them to be happy "in

the Lord," and to "grow strong in the Lord." He called
Tychicus "my loyal helper in the Lord," children are to obey
their parents "in the Lord," and wives to give way to their
husbands "in the Lord." "Keep on working in the Lord's
work always" he tells the Corinthians, "knowing that, in the
Lord, you cannot be laboring in vain." (He uses the phrases
"in Christ Jesus," "in the Lord Jesus" and other similar ones in
the same way.) Clearly, when he told widows they should
remarry only "in the Lord" he was doing more than merely
disapproving of mixed marriages.

That one phrase, "in the Lord," refers to a whole range
of human relationships and occupations, which are all one
relationship and occupation. There is a new life, which entails new attitudes to, and in, old relationships, and carries
new responsibilities and demands. To work "in the Lord" is
utterly different from just working for a living, to obey "in
the Lord" is an act of which obedience out of fear or mere
duty is the barest travesty. So, to marry "in the Lord" means
to enter on a familiar relationship, yet also one which is quite
new, instinct with possibilities, opening out to vast horizons.
And yet this happens not *in spite of* the traditional human institution but *in* it, in the same way that to work, or be happy,
or strong, in the Lord means a transformation, not an alternative. Marriage "in the Lord" is a new creation: one is
called, as all followers of Jesus, to a heroic role.

That means, clearly, that the social and historical context of marriage (and work and family, etc.) is important,
because that is where it all happens, that is where people are
"in the Lord." At any one time and in any one society, to be
married "in the Lord" has some possibilities and not others
(the transformation symbolized by the romantic myth being
one of those possibilities). This is why the awakening of the
hero in marriage at this time is not merely a matter of theology. The hero was always there, if allowed to appear, because being "in the Lord" means that Christ the hero (among
all the other Christs — bridegroom, victim, food, king, child)
is part of our spiritual identity. But at some times any of

these possibilities have more scope than at others. Which ones
can best develop depends on circumstances.

Ours are circumstances in which most of the traditional
social slots for heroes are temporarily discredited. Priests,
scientists, explorers, even revolutionaries, like the elder sons
in the fairy tales, are not adequate to the quest. Professional
churchmen suffer from the past failure of the churches, the
scientific establishment fails out of a similar blinding pride,
explorers tend to be heavily subsidized by big business, and
many leaders of new nations of oppressed minorities turn out
to repeat all the mistakes of those they seek to supplant. Marriage, sitting in the kitchen like Cinderella, truly a traditional
"youngest son" of the old tales, waits to be called on as a last
resort, because no one else is left to run the risks, to "give
and hazard all he hath," as Portia's leaden casket demanded.

That, after all, is what Christians getting married are
required to do. To give and hazard all we have is the basic
demand on Christians, and on Christians in marriage in their
own way. The hazard is great, at present, and it is not so surprising if the courage that can enable people to marry "in
the Lord" is capable of taking them into a hero quest, if that
is what is required by their historical situation.

*   *   *

At present, we need heroes of a particular kind. Solitary
adventures into new realms of earth or of the mind are always
needed, but they are not enough. There is an especial need,
now, for the heroism of a new kind of pioneering; the creation of stable foci for the renewal and continuance of a proper
human life.

In a time when the sheer size of the units into which
human beings are organized oppresses and even kills, when
loneliness is probably the greatest emotional problem, when
people lose hope because nothing they can do seems to be able
to stem the slow, crushing progress of vast governmental and
corporation machines, there is one tiny, tough, and obvious
institution which can resist the monsters and recreate human-
sized units, simply because, whatever its faults, it is a basic

biological fact which can be broken up only by brute power, and never for very long.

When the first reaction came against the exclusive closed family of the last century, the call was to come out, take on outside work, let the children be independent, learn responsibility young, make wide relationships. But if a self-sufficient family circle is liable to neglect the rest of the world, a scattered one is probably neglecting not only the rest of the world but its own members as well. What is required is to use the natural closeness of marriage and family, not as a circle, but as center — the center of a rediscovery for many people of friendship, interdependence, personal care and concern, a sense of belonging *somewhere*.

Families are "naturally" like that, if they develop properly. To say this is, of course, to beg a lot of questions about the way families distort relationships, oppress, confine and so on: such aberrations, however, *are* aberrations. The meaning of being "in the Lord" is that the "natural nature" of marriage and family life can be worked at and, as it were, set free to be itself, and its inmost self is "the Lord." Marriage, at this juncture of history, is just about the only kind of social unit with the power of regeneration, the one that can be a focus of new beginning for many disoriented and demoralized people.

Not too many at a time. That is part of the heroism of marriage. It is about face-to-face relationships, taking their center and meaning from one particular and profound relationship. Smallness is part of the healing process. One of the most marked symptoms of the Western disease is giantism (for enormous numbers are not just more people, but acquire a kind of huge, stupid and damaging corporate personality, of which the fairy-tale "giants" are the symbols). So the right medicine resembles the bottle which Alice found at the bottom of the rabbit hole. Alice had to experiment with shortening and enlarging medicines to find the right size for her circumstances. Scale is important.

Huge cities, huge buildings, huge states, huge busi-

nesses —all these can dwarf people and make them feel helpless and despairing and lonely. To inflate one's ego to match
them only compounds the horrors. To begin to find a way
forward we need to rediscover the harmony of a scale which
is human — in buildings, in farms, in work units, in social
and governmental units.

A generation ago, people talked of world government,
and bigger meant better. Now, more and more small nations
clamor for independence, and people will die rather than be
absorbed and blotted out by their powerful neighbors. Neighborhood, locality, my own people, village, countryside, street,
trade — we need a manageable scale of relationships, people
and places we belong to, our own. Families (and usually only
families) can provide that place which is your own, the people who are your own, where you belong.

A marriage is, after all, the smallest possible social unit,
at least if it is the monogamous kind. (I think we can forget
for now the people who talk about the benefits of polygamy,
which is not really relevant to the West anyway.) But it is a
social unit, even before it is increased by children. Whatever
else may crumble, and until they are all dead, there will be
men and women, and they will pair off and make a life
together.

For a marriage to embody the hero myth, the couple
must dedicate themselves, not simply to each other, but to
work together at something greater than themselves, greater
than their love, or any love they could ever imagine. The hero
requires only goodwill and courage, yet he is, in all the stories,
absolutely essential to the salvation of the people. Unless the
hero succeeds, the people die. He does not have to be emotionally well-developed; he has only to do what needs to be
done. To be married "in the Lord" implies such a commitment. Within it, the romantic myth has its place in developing
the mutual dedication which is indeed a part of marriage, but
its intensity and importance vary greatly.

As a matter of observation, the most successful marriages
are often those in which husband and wife are engaged to-

gether on some undertaking that matters to both. It can be something quite little, like keeping a store, or running a small farm, or simply the business of bringing up the children. Some people, for instance, are just very good at being parents, and make it their whole life as far as possible, and often absorb other children into the family in the process.

In the past, when people expected to have to stick at a marriage, even if it turned out difficult, there were many marriages which were not the oppressive prison that romantic novelists evoke (though undoubtedly there *were* plenty like that). In many cases people rubbed along with contentment and even happiness in a marriage where there was little profound contact, because that little was a common involvement in a way of life. The traditional farmer's wife, for instance, up at dawn and working all day, bearing and rearing children, lined and grey at 40 but tough as hickory, was not really pitiable, even if her marriage relationship was sexually routine and emotionally unexciting by romantic standards. If her husband was often out of temper or unreasonable when the weather was bad or prices down, she put up with it because life was like that. They often reached a plateau of comfortable friendliness and even a deep warmth in old age.

I am not suggesting that this is a better kind of marriage than one worked at in marriage encounter groups. The criteria are quite different. The point is that the qualities that make people stick out a hard life together, not stopping too much to wonder if they are fulfilled, are the qualities people need if they are to develop the hero in marriage, which is what being married "in the Lord" is about.

*   *   *

The vocation of marriage at this time, then, is a vocation of building and making, counseling, encouraging, planning, fighting, enduring. But this raises the question, why married people? Why not any group of people with the right motivation? They are certainly not excluded, but the special importance of married couples in this role at this time is, as so often, both practical and symbolic. Marriage "means" belonging, fidelity, the creation of a new human unit with a definite orientation to the future. It doesn't have to decide on having this kind of character, as some other groups might decide. It just has it, though of course it can fail to live by it. It has it, and everyone recognizes this, even those who feel cynical about marriage as an institution. There has never been a human society, however easy its divorce regulation, that did not assume that stability was the norm, divorce an unfortunate necessity. Because it has this character it is already potentially a center of future life, but in order to become actually one it has to know its own meaning. It has to be aware of the significance of living "in the Lord" in marriage, thus inwardly transforming the "natural" human structure of a family to become fully itself. It has to see in the light of this how exactly fitted for the present hero role marriage is.

A European missionary, who had spent most of his adult life in Africa and 10 years in a newly independent African state, was recalled to work in London, and after a year expressed his profound depression at precisely those features of modern life on which we tend to congratulate ourselves. Homes for the elderly, orphanages, hostels for young people in difficulties, mental hospitals — we may feel they need improvement but we don't doubt that they are useful. This man was revolted by them, and pointed out that in the poorest of the African villages in which he had lived, such institutions would be inconceivable. Old people lived with their sons and daughters, orphans were taken into another family, the village regarded its young people as a common responsibility and they grew up to take their places in its working, and the sick were cared for at home. The standard of medical care might be primitive but the relationships were properly human. Without rehashing the old arguments about whether institutionalized care is necessary, we can at least notice that it is less and less available in a satisfactory form, unless one has plenty of money. But a married couple and their children and home can absorb an elderly relative, or someone else's elderly relative, or a child in need of a home, or someone in need of a refuge and comfort and care, for a while or permanently. The family then becomes bigger, more inclusive, certainly more difficult to cope with, yet the inclusion of difficulties of a real and obvious kind can evaporate other kinds of difficulties — the feeling of pointlessness, the rejection of home by teenagers who feel their parents' lives are futile, and the dreariness which arises because husband and wife have little in common except a diminishing interest in sex, and the same roof. When both are struggling with other people's problems, their own problems of adjustment suddenly seem either soluble, or else not all that important anyway, compared to their sense of unity of purpose.

Marriages don't exist in a vacuum. There are other families, other people around. Much energy (in every sense) is used by most families in striving to create and maintain a totally separate unit in each household, providing its own facilities for feeding, washing, transport, entertainment, holidays. Now, some families are discovering that it helps to pool resources. It cuts costs and gives more free time, more space, more available skills. Some have taken the next step and combined households, in a larger house or a "village"-type unit, preserving family privacy but sharing a great deal, to the enhancement of family life, especially for the children. What one family cannot do, several can do, and those Christian couples who realize this are already creating a number of such communities of families, undertaking together specific forms of work, such as care of disturbed people, or — in a completely different direction — the reclamation and development of neglected farmland. They are making it more productive by methods which permanently enhance the fertility of the soil, and its power to feed people. The kind of long-term dedication which is needed to build up practical, skilled farming, finding the best ways to feed more people without exhausting the soil, is exactly the kind of work that the "nature" of marriage implies, for it involves stability, and an orientation to the future — but a future for *people,* includ-

ing children, to live and grow in, from generation to generation. (My own family, with others, is doing this kind of
thing, besides an educational orientation in particular for
"deprived" youngsters.)

Apart from these general areas where married heroes
are needed, there are as many others as there are particular
forms of service which can be helped by the living out of marriage in the Lord.

* * *

There is one quality above all which is demanded by the
hero role, and which is stressed in the concept of marriage
(or indeed any other relationship or work) in the Lord. That
is fidelity.

Fidelity is an idea that has been angrily criticized, because it seems to contradict the undoubted fact that people
develop and change, and what they long to do at one stage
they find repulsive at a later one. From the point of view of
the romantic myth this is a valid criticism, for what counts
here is the exploration of the depths by intensity of experience,
and that is hard to get sexually with one person over a long
period. The romantic myth, in fact, is to do with intensity
and not with continuity. But from the point of view of the
hero myth, fidelity is of the essence. The hero tales always
involve endurance, and the determination to complete the
quest, however long it takes, however violent the change of
fortune, and however desperate the predicaments in which
the quester is involved. To realize this is to discover a quite
new rationale for the much criticized demand for sexual
exclusiveness and lifelong fidelity in marriage. Extramarital
sex may provide new romantic intensity in a life which has
lost meaning, but it simply rules out the quest. To turn aside
from the quest, as many would-be heroes do in the tales, in
order to explore delicious gardens, taste exquisite meals, wander in elegant castles or enjoy gorgeous maidens, is to show a
failure to understand the nature of the quest. A hero who
does this is, literally, a nonstarter. The real hero knows —

and is constantly being reminded by a series of old women, hermits, talking horses and other embodiments of ancient wisdom — that fidelity is the first, and almost the only, condition of the quest. He also knows that the alternatives which offer themselves en route will be attractive and apparently very important, yet they are to be resisted. The temptations of Jesus have, among others, this obvious significance. To succumb to them means, at best, a long hard struggle to get free and return to the true road.

This is, in practice, the normal experience. The emotional alternatives which offer themselves in the course of any marriage (and not all of them are sexual) may appear — and be — more beautiful, more fulfilling, than the commitment to this particular marriage. But it is in this particular marriage, if it is undertaken "in the Lord," that the hero will set out on his quest. (This assumes that marriage is *entered into* "in the Lord" — that is, with care, thought, prayer and sufficiently long and large knowledge of each others' views and ideals to secure a common ground of hope and determination. Failed marriages *do* happen, but sometimes making something of a difficult one is what the heroism is about.) I have suggested a few of the forms this quest may take. They all involve the single-minded dedication, together, which the hero symbol implies and the gospel demands. For the New Testament contains little (but enough) in its references to marriage to define the purpose of the symbol best known to us in the romantic myth — the bridal symbol of wooing, separation, reunion — whereas the hero is apparent everywhere. This symbol is the expression of the whole Church's being, its type of attitude and action "in the Lord," and, within this, marriage is also transformed in the same image. It does not necessarily cease to be marriage as commonly understood and accepted at the particular historical moment, but it is, at the same time, transfigured from within. Thus marriage in the early Church acted as a focus of the new life, a place to meet (not just a room but *somebody's* room — a home) to learn, to worship, to take refuge, a missionary center

and a point for the distribution of supplies for the needy and
mail for travelers. When the new Church wanted a framework to define its activities it used that of family life — stable,
generous and faithful.

How does this emphasis on dedication *together* combine
with the familiar emphasis on dedication to each other? This
is a matter of practical psychology. People who are working
together at something demanding, if they are open with each
other, come very quickly to a sensitive understanding. This
happens when people work as a team at anything. To do it
well they have to become so immediately aware of each other's
reactions, their strengths and weaknesses, the kinds of abilities
they share and those in which they must balance or com-
pensate for each other, that they can almost be said to "be"
each other. In marriage, this delicate and practical adjustment and cooperation goes on in all aspects of life, though in
some more than others in each marriage, and the level of
sexual learning and celebration is integrated with all the rest.
There may well be blocks that prevent this full integration, but
the visible, tangible everyday fact of a common dedication to
something greater than themselves takes much of the anxiety
out of coping with such blocks, and makes possible the patience and good humor and trust which may gradually lead
to "unblocking."

In conclusion, we can sum up the rationale of the shift
in thinking about Christian marriage under headings of symbol, psychology, sociology and spirituality. The hero *symbol* is
needed to give meaning and purpose in a culture whose myths
have all gone wrong. The old king is sick; the courtiers
quarrel among themselves and oppress the people; neighboring emperors prepare to invade, dragons emerge and ravage
the land; ogres take their pick of the fairest among the children. (I won't bother to attach the allegorical names to
modern examples; it is very easy and you can do it yourself
if you like.) The king's eldest sons, brashly confident in their
methods, promise quick solutions and go forth splendidly
caparisoned to restore peace and prosperity (by which they

mean nobody being allowed to disagree with them, and lots of money for the rich). They return distraught and disheveled and disgraced. (Attach names if you like. As I said, it's easy.) Nobody is left to serve the people, except the youngest son, whom nobody thinks about. His qualities are unfashionable, his habits undistinguished, his friends old-fashioned, his education limited. When he is finally asked to see what he can do, he sets off in a ridiculous state of under-preparedness, with a scraggy old horse, a packet of sandwiches and some obscure advice from his ancient and probably half-witted nurse (this is no doubt how the Church appears to many), who hobbles out of her dusty corner to give him her blessing. But everyone knows what happens afterwards.

Psychologically, marriage needs a morale booster. Married people are tired of being exhorted to improve their marriage, and young people thinking about marriage are uninspired by the spectacle of middle-class couples agonizing over their emotional health when they aren't agonizing over the price of gas and vacations. A different emphasis, a new demand (a very old one, of course, but new to us) is needed and it is not artificially invented as a cure for a sick institution, rather it emerges from the nature of the times and the nature of the institution. Like all really basic human arrangements it has this power of regeneration.

Economically, shortages are increasing and will increase. The dream of affluence for all is over. People have to find ways of living that are decent but simpler, often drastically simpler. The wastefulness of romantic-based marriage is enormous. It expects each couple to be a world unto itself — equipped with all modern conveniences — in which to develop feelings properly. (Look at the ads of couples on thick carpets, listening to expensive stereo sets and eating chocolates, or drinking some very chic brandy. It's expensive to be romantic, and essentially exclusive. One couple, one private world.) The hero, however, although he likes his privacy (or *hers,* for fairy tales are full of female heroes, though they must be distinguished from the princess, who has a different role), is content to muck in with others on the journey and accept conditions as he finds them. Economically, the hero marriage makes much better sense.

Socially, this approach to marriage is one of the few possibly hopeful phenomena. I have described this already, and it is worth thinking about a great deal, if only because *most people in the world marry,* and it seems a terrible waste, to put it mildly, not to draw on such a potential for the renewal of a sick society and the care and support of the principal sufferers from that sickness — the children, the old, the inadequate.

Spiritually, we need hope. Rightly, the people who first realized the facts have hammered at the themes of pollution, exhaustion of natural resources, ecological damage, the ridiculous wastefulness of our use of energy, and of food, and so on. "Doom talk" was needed, but it can be self-defeating. If things get to seem so bad that there is no chance of doing anything about it, we might as well eat, drink and be merry, for tomorrow we die. The doom-talk people are basically right, though sometimes guilty of exaggerations for the sake of effect, but for the warnings to be useful we need hope of a way through. Marriage provides such a hope, for as long as there are people loving and working together, and bringing up children, there is a chance of new life. To take conscious hold on that life, to realize oneself at the heart of it, for others also, is a tremendously vitalizing spiritual experience.

Perhaps, in preparations for marriage, in thinking about the future, in trying to integrate "career" and life, in opening up a future for the children, we can begin here. Let us call up the youngest son from the kitchen corner, rouse him from his dreams and send him out on the quest. He goes in the Lord and he will succeed.

8.The Power of the Promise
Margery Frisbie

After graduating from Mundelein College in Chicago and working for a while as a chemist, Margery returned to Mundelein to become public relations director. That was fortunate because I was working as a newspaper reporter at the time. She was at Mundelein for me to meet when my editor sent me there on an assignment. If she had still been concocting bad odors and burning holes in her lab coat as an industrial chemist, the kind of episode that would have attracted a newspaper's attention might have been fatal. Or I easily could have missed her in the confusion with the fire trucks and all.

Margery has always written. Her first book, Help Your Child Enjoy Books, *grew out of her columns reviewing children's books for the* National Catholic Reporter. *For many years, she wrote a weekly column in the* New World, *which had a wide following, judging from the number of people at gatherings of Catholics who identified me as Margery Frisbie's husband.*

Among the projects we worked on together, besides having eight children, were serving on the board of the Cana Conference of Chicago and editing their publication back in the 1950's.

She served a term as family life chairman for the National Conference of Catholic Women and is at present a member of the family committee of the Illinois State Status of Women Commission. Speaking as an outsider, I think the NCCW offered a better deal — meetings in places like New Orleans and Washington, D.C. The state committee tends to have meetings in Springfield, Illinois — at 8 o'clock in the morning.

This may sound as if she's gone a lot. Not so. Margery likes to garden, indoors and out, and cook and entertain. She has time to talk to children and friends — and to me.

If all the subjects we have to talk about were arranged alphabetically like an encyclopedia, we wouldn't be much past G or H although we've been at it by the hour — to the considerable enrichment of the tea industry — since 1950.

Richard Frisbie

8. The Power of the Promise

A quarter of a century I've looked at marriage from the inside out (and from the inside in). And still I marvel at what fidelity has wrought. Richard's promise 25 years ago to be faithful until death do us part has made it possible for me to be me.

His fidelity has confirmed my striving, my stumbling, my struggles, my advances. Without it, I think the best part of me would have shrunk and faded, the worst might have stretched and swollen. For my most human impulses, my direct responses to experience, have not been cut down and left to wither. They have been protected by the knowledge that there is another who accepts them for what I mean them to be and accepts me as I am. At least most of the time.

To illuminate if not elucidate: the past comes back to each of us in pictures, scenes, memories of elevated intensity. Whenever I nip an anise seed from the back of a ripening springerle, for instance, I'm pulled back to a long-remembered kitchen of a Christmas past.

That licorice tang returns me to a familiar home of my childhood. My friend Junie's grandmother is looking at us over the tops of her slipping spectacles as she presses flat anise seeds onto her cookies' buttered backs. "You know," I hear her saying, pushing up her glasses with the back of a floury hand, "I can remember doing this with my grandmother and thinking how very old she looked. Now I'm the grandmother but I don't feel any different inside than I did when I was that 16-year-old."

We stare in disbelief at her grey bun, her hands white with flour and brown with liver spots. How can such an old woman feel like a 16-year-old inside? How can she claim life in the old girl yet?

What Junie's grandmother was trying to tell us, I think now, was that in spite of her outward appearances she was still an alive, expectant, responsive, aware person, that she hadn't retired into the winter of life. What I'd like to suggest by this side-glance into her redolent kitchen is that she had remained alive because of her relationships.

Someone, some people, were faithful to her.

Now tardily, these many years later, I too believe in the 16-year-old within her, the princess hidden in the crone. For now I have experienced the power of fidelity. And when youngsters around me respond to their expectations of what a woman who has lived half a century should be like, I squelch a saucy impulse to say, "You should know."

Thanks to my relationship with a faithful friend, my princess, too, is functioning, my power to grow and learn and experience, taste of life, savor new sensation, exult in my daily round. This is so because there is one who believes — believes on days when I find it difficult — that there is a spirit in me, as there was in Junie's grandmother, that is uniquely me, uniquely likeable, that is still growing.

This fidelity to me as I am has given me the freedom to reach out in spite of the risks, the necessary blunders and injuries, misjudgments and missteps which are a part of maturing.

Any person who is affirmed by another who is there to his thereness, who is responsive to what he is feeling, who gives him a base from which he can act instead of react, can reach out from that base to "be about his Father's business."

He is liberated by that fidelity which is a presence sustained by a promise which is in turn undergirded by a premise.

The presence is that delicate, devoted attention one person can give another, that permanent state of being turned toward his innermost truest spirit, his potential, his goals, his feelings, his failings, his understanding of himself and others.

The promise is the seriously considered, strenuous willingness to retain that posture of presence no matter what provocation arises to tempt a person to turn his back.

The premise — ay, there's the rub — reveals that it is possible to keep the promise even if "for better" turns out to be "for worse" because all life calls us to die to ourselves. For it is in dying to ourselves, as we so often affirm verbally, that we rise to eternal life.

It is not astonishing that the "I do's" sealing the promise of presence sound bittersweet to those who throng the pews on wedding days. Wedding guests of any age know how often circumstances turn out to be for worse. Forced as they are to acknowledge that every marriage entails a dying to self, the witnesses to each new promise fear an unfair burden on one partner and pray that the necessary dying to self comes in bearable mutual sharing and not in vitiating inequity for the young person on whose side of the church they sit.

I shivered for a guest, not the bride, at a wedding of a favored niece recently. Late for the ceremony, I'd taken a seat at the back of the aged baroque church. A cousin with a better excuse than I (she'd come in from out of town), also late, slipped into the pew behind me, her face bobbing at the back of my head.

Her greeting erupted like a cork from a champagne bottle. "Would you believe," she sputtered into my ear, "that my therapist told me that I married an alcoholic for excitement?"

Ah, I thought, you've been brooding during your long train ride about a marriage, but not about our sweet niece's. And no wonder, considering the miserable dance you've

waltzed with that twinkle-toed young man you married so
hastily out of college.

As I shook my head to indicate the required, "No, I
couldn't believe that you could have married Mark for excitement" (although in reality I could), I inadvertently recalled
the long line of personable young men who had once wooed
this indignant, attractive, middle-aged woman seething at my
ear. She'd passed over any number of suitors before she had
chosen the man whose drinking excesses she was no longer hiding from us, men who were going into their fathers' businesses
or were the first in their families in the professions.

Their dependability and predictability didn't provide the
challenge that attracted her to the young writer whom his
parents called Mark. "They should have called him Question
Mark," her parents commented early in the romance as they
speculated whether this would be a Saturday night when he
would turn up at eight with roses or 12 hours later with
apologies.

They were appalled at his habits but, as Ogden Nash
once wrote about a similar type, Mark "was very resourceful
at being remorseful." My cousin found his apologies sincere,
the making-up heady and the subsequent evenings spon-
taneous, full of activity and exquisite attention.

During one of the making-up periods she persuaded her
reluctant parents that there should be a wedding within the
month. And now here she was, 35 and suffering, admitting
finally what the erratic courtship had presaged: that the
thirst for excitement on her side had been matched by an
equal (though different) thirst on his, that she had been
victimized by both.

She's too late for an observation that Richard and I
often make over a late evening sherry, that one often must
choose in one's friends (and spouses are the best of friends)
between fidelity and emotional adventuring.

One of our neighbors is clear that she became less of a
party personality as she grew more sensitive to others' social
needs. "When I was younger," she says, "I had a reputation

for being a lightning thinker, quick on the uptake and fast on bons mots. But when I began to understand that others needed me to respond to the emotional content as well as the literal meaning of their words, I discovered that I could no longer be quick on the comeback.

"I've lost my reputation for the rapid riposte."

"Lucky for me," her husband says, for he believes that his happiness derives from the personality change reflected in her switch from phrase-maker to homemaker. "Not that I mean that as a put-down," he's quick to insist. "I'm not keeping Jean barefoot and pregnant. On the contrary, she's been an executive most of our life together and we've shared responsibility for Jamie.

"People don't have to hug the sink to be homemakers. They have to hug each other. What I mean is that they have to see that creating a home for themselves and for others is as important a vocation as any other.

"In fact," he says, "in that sense I'm as much a home-maker as Jean. It's our choice and style."

This kind of faithfulness to a promise, based as it is on consistency to self and availability to the other, is the root from which happy lives seem to spring. It doesn't depend on the traditional role of the woman as the one expected to understand, to foster affection, to give of herself in a spirit of sacrifice. Rather, both partners choose as a high good a life of faithful solicitude toward each other and their children.

Persons who don't want to be doggedly faithful or even sheltered by a loyal affection suggest that humankind's peer-less works of art have been created without that kind of fidelity.

In the economy of life it does seem necessary to separate the spirit of devotion that is needed to create a unique master-piece and that kind which makes living the highest art. Syn-dicated columnist Sydney J. Harris explains this by saying that a man's creative work is what "he aspires to; his personal relations are (generally, not always, of course) what he is unable or unwilling to change in the convolutions of his personality." He cites Bertrand Russell who could write splendidly on marriage and be a rotten husband, Dorothy Sayers whom Harris would have liked to have met until he read her biography, *Such a Strange Lady,* and Beethoven who alienated all.

People like these who are off-base at a psychic level can fire out a universal message that transcends their pain and unites them with suffering humanity everywhere. But they can't seem to create happy lives. Possibly that's what Tolstoy meant when he said that all happy families are happy in the same way but that each unhappy family is unhappy in its own individual way. Happy families are faithful; their happiness is inescapably linked to their virtues.

When Jefferson wrote in the Declaration of Independence of the pursuit of happiness, he meant it in the sense of the ancient Greeks as a "life well-lived or a good life as a whole." William Gorman and Mortimer Adler amplify this concept in *The American Testament* when they suggest that true happiness depends upon the possession of moral values. "If [an individual] fails to acquire them, he alone is to blame. No organized society or instituted government can confer moral virtue upon him or make him a man of good moral character."

You see the importance of the virtue of faithfulness in relationships when C. S. Lewis could write in *Surprised by Joy* that once his mother had died he was to experience moments of surpassing joy but that "settled happiness was gone forever." His mother had provided the center from which he could sally forth and to which he could safely return, always certain of a welcome. His father withdrew from his sons after the death of his wife.

That "joy" which Lewis knew was close to the transport of "falling in love."

I caught a glint of that emotional glow recently as I drove past a young couple on the shoulder of the road by a nearby shopping center. In the moment their image broke against my retinas I was aware of their easy intimacy, their heedless incorporation of all the rapture in the world into the moment they were sharing. They were oblivious to all of us passing by, he trundling his bike, astride the seat but walking it slowly, she swinging her knitted hat, rhythmically brushing against his shoulder.

We ought to package moments like that, I thought, spin a cloak around them. Then I realized that this is part of what marriage is, an attempt to institutionalize the shining moments. It's an acknowledgment that the gift those two were sharing is worth saving. How long would it last even for them? By the time I was stacking tomato sauce and peanut butter on my shelves was she carping at her mother that dinner was late and that she'd never have time to wash her hair? Was he slinking into the basement to get out of sweeping the drive?

For the peak moments of communion and ecstasy are ringed about by all the spells when we're annoyed or annoying, badgered or badgering, frustrated or frustrating.

That's the "for better" and the "for worse" of marriage; we bring ourselves when we cross the threshold. Too often we wed thinking of the better. We don't have an early warning system to inject realism into our jubilant plans.

In *The Sixth Directorate,* an absorbing spy story which turns on obedience to the Communist party, Joseph Hone's heroine carries her initial commitment through parlous hazard and perilous incident. "If you are serious," her recruiter had told her in her early idealistic stage, "you will put up with every setback. And they'll come, be sure of that — the public disappointments and, much worse, the personal loss of faith. And when they do, remember the choice, the decision you make now; that you believe these ideas we've talked about are right. And nothing should really change that."

We don't find it strange that a Communist agent should persevere in the cause or that she should be personally and carefully recruited for her responsibilities. Why is it atypical then to counsel young persons bent on a commitment to each other, which is certainly equally serious, of the sloughs and chasms ahead? Yet the identical sentiments in a wedding sermon — "you can be sure of public disappointments and personal loss of faith" — would frighten participants and guests alike.

If this promise, this pledge to be present during the dark nights of the soul as well as during the shining moments, is alarming, it is also enlarging. A promise creates the person who makes the promise and his partner. It commits the first to a maturing responsibility and protects the other from a Camus-like view of the world as one where all men are strangers, where justice is arbitrary and where human action is without meaning.

Anyone can be in love. But the follow-up, the constant concern for the partner, the will to know his deepest needs, the respect for his freedom to grow his own way and the willingness to take responsibility for him in the sense of responding to his needs as they are discovered: that is a work of a lifetime.

Couples are in an ideal position to be watchfully attentive each to the other. Because each can come to know the other under the protection of a promise to be faithful "until death," learning about each other and being learned about can strain the relationship but it shouldn't destroy it. The learning-by-heart which is the daily lesson of marriage creates the bond.

Again, because each of the partners is looking to the other's needs, each can be free to look past his own hungers to those which transcend the immediate relationship. Each can do this without getting out of touch with his own requirements because he has a partner who is constantly aware of him and who warns periodically, "Look, what you need is . . . ."

Usually it isn't fair to guess what might have been. However, when reading the largely autobiographical *Sons and Lovers,* one can't help feeling that if D. H. Lawrence's mother could have looked to her husband's needs and accepted in him that rough masculinity which initially drew her to him, then she would not have devastated her family.

She chose to despise him, refusing to take him as he was. It is not surprising that in later years Lawrence felt that he had been unfair in his portrait of his father in his early novel. Lawrence came to see his mother's role in edging the earthy miner out of the family circle and installing her sons in a top-heavy arrangement that meant disappointment for all of them. Technically faithful to her promise, she was spiritually destructive, throwing her generation and the next into disarray.

If Lawrence's parents had been present to each other they could have prevented that vinegary outlook common to those whose full gaze is turned back on themselves. No matter how diligent the self-attention of those who look first to their own needs, they can't give themselves that *sine qua non* of happiness, a faithfulness that searches out and fills genuine needs — any more than they can tickle themselves. It takes an "other" to make a person at home in the world.

Lately there's been showing on late night television an old Noel Coward movie about a *Brief Encounter* between an English housewife and an attentive doctor she's met by chance in a railway station in a nearby metropolis. Years ago when I saw the first run in New York City I thought her trysts romantic and sympathized with her plans — finally aborted — to escape her crashingly dull matrimonial state.

Subsequent attention to marital vagaries has convinced me that if Celia Johnson had left her nice husband for the dashing doctor her new relationship would have duplicated the old in short order. She would have been pulling behind the same dusty baggage she had on the shelf at home.

Her challenge wasn't to find a new love, but to put love where there was no love. Celia, instead of concentrating her energies on her brief encounter, could have focused on the man across her hearth whom she already knew as "the most kind and true friend in the world."

The potential for the relationship she craved was in this devoted friend. But it doesn't come easily, this building of a golden room where two can live as one and yet be two. It's constructed of the joys of experiencing the other, but also the pain of those moments when one has revealed a weakness and the other has taken advantage, when one has asked too much and the other has given too little, when one won't accept a "no" and the other won't give a "yes," when physical fatigue has drained civility out of a relationship and when false expectations have blocked attempts at healing.

There are days when it seems that all that is left is the promise. But more is always present — the need.

And to that need attention must be paid.

It isn't fair, however, to those who have struggled with a surfeit of need in themselves, their partners and their children to suggest that under all circumstances it is possible for a person to remain permanently linked by a marriage vow. It is possible to make a valiant effort toward responding to the needs of the partner and yet to find that the effort does not confirm our Christian hope that openness to our spouse, willingness to be forthright with him as he reveals himself, and honesty about our own personal feelings will draw him to wholesome growth.

Although we can agree in principle with philosopher Simone Weil that there is no person so harmed psychically that he cannot be helped, yet any surveyor of the married scene separates that generous axiom from the often intolerable reality of individual marriages. One spouse can struggle valiantly — yet in vain — to make a marriage work.

Sometimes a person must choose between cutting off a relationship or being gradually destroyed by the uncertainty or violence of life with an erratic partner. Sometimes a person must choose between his devotion to the quickening spirits of his children and the overwhelming pull of a partner disoriented to a point where he makes no contribution to the family's needs. A decision put off too long can pull a whole family into an engulfing vortex of emotional ills.

In sorrow, then, that he cannot be all things to all men, a person must decide whether to cut off the needful partner in order to save the limited resources available; whether to staunch what wounds he can; whether to husband his strength for a beginning of healing for all.

No family can fashion a human life for its members without the help of a community, but a shattered family has an increased need for allies.

A community can give a fragile family an accepting, sustaining, reassuring, objective backup which operates out of a long knowledge both of man's perverseness and of his powers of recuperation. It can eschew both fingerpointing and hysterics in its long view of the widespread human desire to escape life's common problems. It can bolster those who are willing to make a long-term commitment to repairing resistant relationships.

Though current conventional wisdom touts immediate satisfaction "so long as no one is hurt," the long sweep of human history and literature suggests that man reserves his highest admiration for those who set themselves the hard tasks in life.

Wherever there has been storytelling — and where has there not been? — human hearts have resonated to stories of faithfulness against odds, the boy with his finger in the dike, "the horn of Roland in the passages of Spain," *fidus Achates,* Ruth amid the alien corn, the king's son Rama in the ancient Indian epic who was true unto his holy promise.

Who could have been a more unlikely candidate for regeneration than Colin in *The Secret Garden* with his agate grey eyes, invalided and hidden from birth, his mother dead, his father fleeing her image in his son's face, stolid servants fearing and spoiling the hysterical child? Yet I returned a hundred times during my childhood to Mary Lennox's first discovery of the phobic sickling in his carved, four-poster bed hung with brocade.

In my need to know that every human being is salvageable — that I was salvageable — I craved the reassurance of Mary's determination that there were life and health for Colin in the secret garden where his mother's spirit was still present.

Colin seemed totally fettered by his circumstances of

birth and isolation. Yet Mary responded to his needs in a
way that freed him to live, to come walking to the great house
with his father in the end, "as strongly and steadily as any boy
in Yorkshire, his eyes full of laughter."

In some sense Mary had entered into the quintessential
human act of laying down her life for her brother, to the
Christian knowledge that whatever we do, we do unto Him.
To Him who is stand-in for the world.

Traditionally we assent to the valor of laying down one's
life in battle, by dying. We hesitate to offer that same respect
to that person who lays down his life for another, by living.

We are unwilling to believe in the power of the promise.
It can take two needful people imbued with the idea that they
can do for each other what they cannot do for themselves
and make of them a whole that is greater than the sum of
the partners. It can also sustain the heroism of one who tries
to heal the world through healing his partner.

Following this promise doesn't bring a person "cheap
happiness," but it does carry with it that happiness which
Jefferson thought was closely linked to virtue.

At the least it gives the person who tries to live by the
promise — however difficult the circumstances — the satisfaction of dedicating his energies to a life-task which will take
his measure. At the most it can mean the conversion of an
unequal relationship into a final rich accord. That is the
time when "for worse" turns out to have been "for better"
after all.

9. A Child To Receive the Kingdom

Thomas L. Shaffer

Tom Shaffer is professor of law at the University of Notre Dame, where he teaches and writes about wills, trusts and taxes, legal counseling, legal education, administrative law, and Christians as lawyers.

Born in 1934, he grew up in a loving, Christian family in the Mountain West (all the other men in three generations of his family have been cowboys). He was married as a teenager (19) to an older woman (20). He served in the Air Force, was graduated from the University of Albuquerque, and studied law, on a scholarship, at Notre Dame. He practiced law for two years in Indianapolis before returning to teach at Notre Dame in 1963. He was dean of law for four years and has been a visiting professor at UCLA and the University of Virginia.

Our eight children, ages 11 to 21, say of their father: He is a smart, sensible, lovable Dad . . . he takes time for us rather than trying to make money all the time, and he's generous . . . he thinks a lot about things . . . a gourmet cook and a scholar . . . warm and considerate . . . he has faith in other people and lets them try things for themselves . . . integrates humanism and Christianity . . . he blends his belief in civil liberties with his Christian thinking and practices.

Tom Shaffer is my best friend and the most interesting person I know — especially when he is trying to figure out something, as in this article.

Nancy Shaffer

169

9. A Child to Receive the Kingdom

Jesus said, "Let the children come to me, and do not hinder them; for to such belongs the kingdom of God. Truly I say to you, whoever does not receive the kingdom of God like a child shall not enter it" (Lk 18:16-17).

Jesus didn't say we have to have children. He seems to have said nothing on that subject at all, except to notice that a mother feels better after her baby is born than she does while it's being born. When he was with children he loved them, but we don't know what he said to them. He talked to adults, but not about the children they have; he talked to adults about the children they were. He talked to adults about being children, to receive the kingdom. The task he gave us was to learn to be the children we already are. It is my idea that we Christian married people have children for that narrow, selfish, gospel reason — so that we will have someone to provide a home for us; to show us how to be the children we are; and to help us receive the kingdom. He said that the homes our children prepare for us already belong to the kingdom.

Driving through Canada last summer, I heard an interview program on the Canadian Broadcasting Company, chaired by an earnest young woman who celebrated with her listeners the freedom from childbirth given by science to her and her contemporaries in nice places like Canada. She interviewed a farm woman who was, I guess, about as old as I am and who may have had as many children as we have.

The farm wife said that she supposed the pill to be a good thing; she was happy about the contraceptive technology available to her daughters. But, she said, she was sad about it, too, because the days were gone when children were allowed to happen.

I thought about the way her children happened, and ours, and also about the way her child had happened. The child that is in each of us used to just happen, too, and doesn't so much anymore. I felt a little sad about the planning that goes into the children we are, and she and I both felt a little sad about the planning that goes into the children we have. The distinction makes some sense when you read about children in the gospels. Jesus seems not to have talked to the child in children. He talked to the child in adults. He said awesome things about the child, laid awesome duties on the adults who carry the child around within them and hide it under layers of urbanity. But he also said that he loved the child.

The children of the Canadian farm woman "had happened." I thought that the child in the farm wife had happened, too, as had the child in her daughter, and the child in me. Her daughter now has to choose the child as much as she has to choose the children, and both things are serious business. The farm wife implied that choosing children has come to have little to do with love, or even with sex.

Science made children a Sartrean dilemma. This woman's daughter, forced to choice, cannot choose not to choose, as her mother could. Progress forced a distinction on the daughter, between the inevitability of her own child and the appearance of companions for her own child. The reality of intimate others in the daughter's life is less automatic than it was for her mother. The Canadian farm wife and I, from

such wisdom as there is in living with the children in each
of us for half a lifetime, hail science, as we should, but we are
wistful, too, maybe because our children cannot know how
things were when science was less helpful. (This is not to
argue about the value of progress — progress is inevitable —
but is to be wistful, a bit, as the farm wife was.)

The farm wife on the CBC was not identified, no
doubt out of respect for her privacy. It occurred to me,
though, that a woman used, as she was used, to illustrate how
quaint mothers have become is just as well left anonymous.
To know her at all well, that is, to know the child she is,
whom Jesus loves, you would have to meet her children.
("Oh," people say to me, "I know you. You're Ed Shaffer's
father.") And meeting her children you might be attracted
to them, and it would be harder to think of them as mistakes
made in the old days.

She was not identified, but I thought of her again when
I read Ken Woodward's *Newsweek* cover story about parents.
Ken reported surveys to the effect that middle-aged Ameri-
cans who have children are happier than middle-aged Ameri-
cans who do not have children. There is, as a matter of
science, a probability that the anonymous woman on the
CBC is better off than her daughters will be. I think she
knew it all along.

*   *   *

When I was a child in Sunday school, in the First Baptist Church, Fruita, Colorado, we sang a song based on the
King James Version of Jesus' words about being children, to
the tune of a Civil War camp song. I later went to Rome,
to college, and to law school. In each of those conversions, I
learned less about how to be a child in the gospel sense and
more about how to be clever. After a quarter of a century
of marriage, blessed with an almost perfect companion, and
with seven sons and a daughter, I am writing about children
in Christian marriage. I think the best way to do that is to
go back to the Sunday school, if I can, and then to sing the
gospel song — back, as Jesus intended, to a self I can love,

who, because he is loved even by himself, can receive the kingdom.

The child is inevitable. As long as I am at all, the child is there. My choosing him is not inevitable, but his being there is. He has been joined by other children — our children — who are our letters of recommendation from Christ: "You yourselves are our letter of recommendation, written on your hearts, to be known and read by all men; and you show that you are a letter from Christ delivered by us, written not with ink but with the Spirit of the living God, not on tablets of stone but on tablets of human hearts" (2 Cor 3:1-3). Our children are now inevitable, too. As long as I am they are, and no less part of me, nor I of them, than my own child is part of me and part of them.

The gospel child is a mystery, as most things in the gospel are, but the world's learning to be clever sometimes illuminates the mystery. The child is the heart of the theories of collective unconscious, and ego and superego in psychoanalytic psychology, the heart of the "ego states" on which Berne and Harris and all the others based transactional analysis, parent effectiveness training, and dancing around the room with an encounter group. It is the child who is able to feel okay, and let other people be okay; it is the child who is born to win. Every one of us, at his clearest and most open, is a child learning how to receive the kingdom.

The conventional ideas on what children are like are manipulations by adults. I have spent more than half my life in the home our children provide me, and I will tell you that the conventional ideas about children are not true. I doubt that Jesus meant conventional ideas when he said "enter like a child." For example, a child is not simple. The children I know are complicated; if I treat them as if they were simple, I act not out of their truth but out of my need for somebody simple to deal with.

Children aren't gullible, or at least not for long. They are not especially trusting; few people in literature are more canny than Huckleberry Finn, and I think Mark Twain had

him right. Children are not more honest than anyone else —
rather less so, in my experience. They lack most of the civilized
virtues, because they lack the weapons we adults use to defend
civilized virtue. Children are not even remarkably innocent,
a point William Faulkner made well in his last novel, *The
Reivers*. In any case, Jesus did not require innocence of those
who are to receive the kingdom.

What Jesus required, I think, was that each of us find
the self whom Jesus loves, the self each of us is able to love,
and to that end he directed our attention to the child within
each of us. He said, "receive the kingdom of God like a child."
This child we have to be is not past. Freud and Jung and
Berne prove that he's been around all along. The gospel
requirement is not a matter of returning to anything; it is a
matter, as Jesus said, of being somebody, somebody each of
us already is, somebody who can be loved, not by the world,
but by himself, by the person whose child he is.

The whole business of children in our lives begins with a
gospel child, before we have any other children. It is, to
begin with, a matter of salvation.

*   *   *

If you want to receive the kingdom, Jesus said, you
have to come to terms with your child. A married person
begins to do that by giving companions to his child. There
are other ways, no doubt, but companionship is the way
married people do it. The other ways are harder. Anyone
who has had a glimpse into the life of a celibate religious
community knows that the other ways are harder. I suspect
but do not know that couples who "wait to have children"
find that the other ways are harder.

I know a thoughtful Christian who says a marriage
which is closed to children is not a Christian marriage at all.
It is a "relationship," as some of our kids say; and they are
probably right in seeing little difference, if a "relationship"
is all that is involved, between marriage and its alternatives.
People are able to respond to one another in "relationships,"
but, my friend says, they are not married until they can

respond to children. He may be right; if he is, I would say that it is because marriage is a way Christians choose to receive the kingdom. Some Christians choose to love the children in themselves by giving children to their children. We call these Christians married.

My friend is radical and stark, but I thought of him as I read, in John Barth's novel *Chimera,* a secular expression of the same idea:

> [S]he took what she was pleased to call the Tragic View of Marriage and Parenthood: reckoning together their joys and griefs must inevitably show a net loss, if only because like life itself their attrition was constant and their term mortal. But one had only different ways of losing, and to eschew matrimony and child-rearing for the delights of less serious relations was in her mind judgment to sustain a net loss even more considerable. Nor, mind, did she regard this perspective (which she applied as well to everything from vacation trips to historical movements) as spiritually negative or bleak: to affirm the antinomy of the cosmos, which antinomy she took to be not absurd contradiction but rich paradox, the pity and terror of the affirmation whereof effected in the human soul an ennobling catharsis (Random House, 1972).

Barth has the woman's husband make these reflections; the husband perceives the joy of children less biologically than his wife does (I know the feeling), but his acceptance of life — of his child and of his children — has some implicit joy in it. Tevye, in *Fiddler on the Roof,* has more: "Life has a way of confusing us, blessing and bruising us . . . a gift we are seldom wise enough ever to prize enough." Life has a value beyond examination; Tevye knows it, and Barth's young woman feels it, and so, if we are lucky, do we Christians. The difference is that a Christian's sense of the "antinomy of the cosmos" has been redeemed. The entropy in all things, the constancy of attrition, has been transformed. God became a child. God is, still, a child.

Tevye's song, and most of the best expressions of Jewish joy, have a sardonic side. Tevye is a man who knows what horror is — more than you or I will ever know. Tevye knows the score — the pogroms, the limited hope for a Jewish family in 19th-century Russia. I have often thought that Tevye's song is a theme for discussion of the horrors of the 1970's— especially the horror of a country which would probably have never come to killing unborn children as a means of birth control if it had not enjoyed too much comfort.

Tevye's song is better for the limited purpose of argument about abortion than the gospel song is. Abortion is not a spiritually apposite part of reflection on the gospel song. It becomes apposite only because we live in a world which learned, somewhere between Auschwitz and Viet Nam, to worship death; it would not otherwise be necessary to pause, in an essay on the family, to suggest that it is improper to kill children, that killing people is not a useful way to solve social and economic problems.

Arguments against killing children may be futile anyway. I have often thought so, as I argued about it. Bolt's Thomas More (*A Man For All Seasons*) said enough about letting children live:

> I do none harm, I say none harm, I think none harm. And if this be not enough to keep a man alive, in good faith I long not to live. . . . My poor body is at the King's pleasure. Would God it might do him some good.

It may be that our generation's endless worry about "relationships," accompanied as it has been by too much comfort, is what leads us into a valley where death is worshiped. In any case a philosophy of "relationship" does not, as a philosophy of marriage does, lead on to the gospel child who is to receive the kingdom.

The trouble with "relationships" is that they prolong adolescence. They don't come to terms with the child; they keep him from growing. Their purposes are all self-referring. The most defensible moral rule on birth control would be one that permitted contraception only after at least one child was born — so that there could be a marriage, rather than a "relationship," and so that the parent's child could be on about the business of preparing to receive the kingdom.

* * *

The point is that children need a home. The gospel child needs a home, and providing children is the married way to build a home for the child. The essence of home is, as Robert Frost's hired man knew, that when you go there they have to take you in; it is something you don't have to deserve. Arnold Morgenstern (father of Herman Wouk's *Marjorie Morningstar*) tries with only partial success to say this, in that moving scene in the rowboat, when Marjorie who has a "relationship" going, says that children are for Catholics. For her, instead, are:

> the finest foods . . . the finest wines, the loveliest
> places, the best music, the best books, the best art.
> Amounting to something. Being well known, being
> myself, being distinguished, being important, using
> all my abilities, instead of becoming just one more
> of the millions of human cows! Children, sure,
> when I've had my life and I'm not fit for anything
> else.

And Arnold, who knows about a home for the child Arnold, says,

> I'll tell you. I think if you're happy those things
> must be nice to have, but if you're unhappy they
> don't help much. The main thing is happiness.
> Love, sure, I agree with you. But love means chil-
> dren (Doubleday, 1955).

Arnold was not, you see, worried about a home for Marjorie's children. He was worried about a home for Marjorie.

It is not the children I have who need the home, but the child I am. Parents don't provide a home; they move into a home provided by the children they bear. When you go there they have to take you in; you don't have to deserve it; and you don't have to fool anybody to get in. The silliest of all silly notions about families is the notion that people qualify to be parents, as they might learn to play tennis or to get a driver's license. Our families are theaters for our salvation. Our business is not to qualify for the kingdom; it is to prepare to receive it. "For if while we were enemies we were reconciled to God by the death of his Son, much more, now that we are reconciled, shall we be saved by his life" (Rom 5:10). My idea is that married Christians prepare to receive the kingdom — that is, to come to terms with the gospel child — by bearing children and coming into the home their children provide for them.

Once the children are on hand, the home becomes almost inevitable; there is not much significant choice after that. There are unwanted children in the world, and I cry for them, but most of the middle-class American talk about unwanted children ranges from sophistry to self-pity. It should be gone when children appear and demand to be wanted. I know, as a matter of extensive clinical experience, that it should be gone, and even when my children make me miserable I know I would be more miserable without them.

We make heavy weather out of being parents. Our cultural weakness for expertise may explain why. It seems to require of us a credential for parenthood, a license or diploma, and then to impose a scoreboard on our use of the franchise. The experts, or our lust for them, make a sacrament sound like craftsmanship, or being an informed voter. An illegitimate verb, "to parent," has been invented to describe it. The verb and the vocation deserve each other.

The ideas of our unenlightened forebears were bad enough — images of the father as a ruthless, unpleasant God. Our enlightened forebears talked us out of projecting the ruthlessness back on God, but they did not provide an ade-

quate model of the unprojected parent who was left over.
They left us insecure, and estranged from the gospel child.
We "fight for our children as if it were heaven itself we have
in mind as we roll up our sleeves or bare our teeth," psy-
chiatrist Robert Coles says.

> If one book fails, or one educational philosophy,
> or one guru's . . . words, we do not become apa-
> thetic or skeptical or wryly amused; we do not turn
> to *ourselves,* and assume our own sovereignty, so
> to speak, as human beings who have a right, even
> an obligation, to hold on to certain ethical prop-
> ositions, beliefs, standards — even at a sacrifice.
> Rather, we become restless, feel dissatisfied with
> someone or something "out there," and immedi-
> ately undertake yet another search.

Parenthood comes out sounding like a recipe for the perfect
martini.

                              *   *   *

Bearing children is one thing; living with them is something else. Tom Braden (in *Eight Is Enough*) reviewed his
fragmented budget and asked his wife how she thought they
were going to live when they grew old, and their children
were gone. And his wife said, "How do you know you'll be
old?" The rueful young husband in Barth's *Chimera* assessed

> the psychological cost of parentage, to ourselves
> individually and to the married relationship: fa-
> tigue, loss of spontaneity, diminishment of ardor,
> general heaviness — a kind of accelerated aging,
> the joint effect of passing years, increased respon-
> sibility, and accumulated familiarity — never al-
> together compensated for by deeper intimacy.

Erma Bombeck makes the same point in the daily newspaper,
and she is funnier. (A Christian is bound, I suppose, to look
at Jesus Christ, and at all of those to whom Jesus gave special

assignments, and then ask by what right he thinks he's en-
titled to an easy life.) My interest here has been to talk
about the prevention and destruction of children (contraception and abortion); I venture into the subject of living with
children only to prove that the babies we allowed to happen
did grow up, and I still live with some of them, and they have
become some of my favorite people.

Conventional ideas about living with children are as
bad as conventional ideas of what children are like. Braden,
Barth and Bombeck realize that, and make an art of scoffing
at the conventional ideas. They are not be taken seriously,
at least not at the level of their words. One's ardor and spon-
taneity tend to diminish, this side of heaven, whether he has
children or not. Because Braden, Barth and Bombeck have
made an art, not of the business of living with children, but
of conventional ideas about it, they are less annoying than,
say, images of parenthood on television. Television parenthood — which many people *do* take seriously — ranges over a
spectrum of about half a degree, from sentimentality of the
Edgar Guest sort, to the worst of scoutmaster condescension,
all of it (now) without regard to race, creed, or color. People
look at it and then feel guilty because life is not like that. It
makes things worse; and it is therefore evil stuff.

The realistic text on living with children is probably
Henry Higgins in *Pygmalion* (the relevant parts of which
were left out of *My Fair Lady*). Eliza Doolittle complained
to Professor Higgins that he failed to treat her as a lady should
be treated. And he said the charge was untrue, that he
treated her as he did everyone else. Living with children —
if one must talk about it as a matter of principle — should
begin with that beginning, because that beginning makes it
clear that children are other people; they are not objects for
our altruism, our instruction, or our guilt about making too
much money.

The first reality is a kick from the other side of a mother's
tummy. The kick says that somebody else is there. My friend
and teacher Bob Rodes had the same insight Shaw had, and

Bob, who has inspired much of this essay, baptized it and
applied it to his children: "Only a handful of traditional
values are genuinely religious," he said. "I would not say I
'inculcate' them in my children. I bear in my house such
witness to them as I can."

My children, like all of the other people I meet, are
Christ in the world. The difference is a difference of intensity
and a blessing. I live with them more. They know me better
than anyone. And — the blessing — they love me anyway.
"Love does not rejoice in what is wrong. Love rejoices in the
truth" (1 Cor 13:6). They give me a home; I don't have
to deserve them. And from that beginning I can make such
friendships with them as I am able to make; I am free to
bear witness to the gospel, but not free — not even able, thank
God — to substitute my views for theirs, or — as seems implicit in a culture bent on "parenting" — their views for mine.
I can hope that they will help me come to terms with the
gospel child. I know they are more likely to help me than
anyone else is — which is why God put me among them —
but there are no warranties.

There is a frightening and beautiful truth here. It is
really possible to be known well and loved. There is an affec-
tive depth, almost impossible to describe, to the knowledge a
child has about his parent. His reception, when you notice
him watching you closely, is oppressively sensitive. Robert
Pirsig, in *Zen and the Art of Motorcycle Maintenance,* made
a compelling subtheme out of this point. The journey in that
story is a father-son journey. The father has been a mental
patient; his memory had been eradicated with electricity. The
journal is a search for his former (and future) self; it is like
a search for the former (and future) gospel child. But the
son is not searching for his father's self; it is present to him,
present, even, as part of him. He knows, as he watches his
father search, and he feels and tries to express compassion for
his father. The barrier to compassion which has to come
down is put up by the father, who hasn't found himself yet,
and who is frightened in the search. Living with children is

like that; and the blessing, so usual that it takes great effort to prevent it, is that the child loves you anyway. It is the child who provides the home.

The world commits my children to my dominance. That is a matter of worldly convenience. It had, traditionally, an economic end; it is better explained now, at least in the comfortable countries, as a matter of competence: parents have control of children because most of us feel that parents produce better results than anyone else is likely to produce. In the Amish school case, the Supreme Court held that parents are free to deny their children even the benefits of education, benefits most of our society regards as more sacred than anything, if it regards anything as sacred. A more obviously sacred reason for the result — a reason the Court might have emphasized, but did not — is protection for the greatest comfort life has, the comfort of accepting and being accepted by other people. Law cannot create that comfort, but it occasionally has the good sense to leave alone those who do create it.

Law, at least, and better than most of the rest of our culture, preserves a sense of the importance of origins: "Hearken unto me, ye that follow after righteousness, ye that seek Jehovah: look into the rock whence ye were hewn, and to the hole of the pit whence ye were digged" (Is 51:1). The gospel child is there.

The gospel mandates a certain minimum amount of Christian society. "He will gather us all together" (Eph 1:10). Families are doubtless the most common and most natural response to the mandate. When Jesus said that we can have what we ask the Father for, provided we ask it together, he was not stating a liturgical condition (although I once thought so); he was insisting that we invite someone else to bear the pain or joy or fear that drives us to prayer. He wanted us to do his work for him, the work of being Christ in the world, and he knew that the hard part of compassion is not giving comfort but asking for it.

He knew that, *for an adult,* the hard part of compassion is asking for it. "Men seldom tell the truth of what is in them, even to their dearest friends," Anthony Trollope noticed. "They are ashamed of having feelings, or rather of showing that they are troubled by any intensity of feeling. It is the practice of the time to treat all pursuits as though they were only half important to us, as though in what we desire we were only half in earnest." His example was Sir Roger Scatcherd, who "had plenty of friends . . . in the parliamentary sense . . . but he had no friend who could sit with him over his own hearth . . . and moderate the sighings of the inner man" (*Doctor Thorne*, 1858).

Compassionate friendship, being "visibly eager," Trollope said, "seems childish." Children know how to cry, how to ask for compassion, and they are — until the world really gets to them — not shy about asking. Which is, of course, the point. A child who is ready for the kingdom knows how to ask for help. He knows that he has few alternatives. We who have children may be learning from them how to be able to pray as St. Matthew's Jesus told us to pray. Love grows out of the common lot that a parent has with his children. As Father Henri Nouwen said,

> Sometimes, a father or mother will be honest and free enough to say that he or she looked at the new baby as at a stranger without feeling any special affection, not because the child was unwanted but because love is not an automatic reaction. It comes forth out of a relationship which has to grow and deepen. We can even say that the love between parents and children develops and matures to the degree that they can reach out to each other and discover each other as fellow human beings, who have much to share and whose differences in age, talents and behavior are much less important than their common humanity (*Creative Ministry*, Doubleday, 1973).

How are Christians to live among one another? St. Paul (Rom 12) says,

> Let us have a warm affection for one another as be-
> tween brothers, and a willingness to let the other
> . . . have the credit. . . . When trials come, endure
> them patiently; steadfastly maintain the habit of
> prayer. Give freely to fellow Christians in want,
> never grudging a meal or a bed to those who need
> them. And as for those who try to make your life
> a misery, bless them. Don't curse, bless. Share the
> happiness of those who are happy, and the sorrow
> of those who are sad. Live in harmony with one
> another. Don't become snobbish but take a real
> interest in ordinary people. Don't become set in
> your own opinions. Don't pay back a bad turn by
> a bad turn to anyone.

It is hard to live that way anywhere, and I fail at it more often than not, but it comes as a surprise to think that it might count for me to live that way toward my own children. With a few exceptions (trials, miseries, and opinions), I don't find it especially hard to live in some kind of harmony with them — to have warm affection toward them, not grudge them meals and a bed, to bless them and share their happiness, and to live, if not in greater peace with them than with others, at least in more honesty. On the whole, I do better at all of this inside my house than outside it; it is not easy anywhere, but it's easier here than elsewhere. I think it does count here. It does, at least, once we get rid of the idea that we must search scripture for new ways to feel guilty, and get hold of the idea that being a child, to receive the kingdom, may involve new reasons for feeling good. Bob's idea about bearing witness among one's children relates, I think, in a radical and comforting way, to my boyhood Baptist song. "Jesus loves the little children of the world," we sang in Sunday school. "Red and yellow, black and white. All are precious in his sight." And I am, among my own children, feeding them and blessing them, also one of the children Jesus loves.

The object, I think, is to offer my children what I am bound to offer anyone — accord, comfort, sacrifice, as these

come from our common human nature and from the brother-
hood due one who has, because of the new dispensation, been
found innocent. The difference between my children and
everyone else is that it is easier to bear witness among them,
easier to give and seek compassion among them, easier to pray
with them, easier to be like a child — that's what Jesus said,
"like a child" — in their society. And so, I confidently hope,
easier to receive the kingdom.

The Photographer
Stephen Moriarty

I think Stephen is a wonderful old trunk filled with child-hood coin collections, arrowheads from his grandparents' farm in Georgia, obscure books, Carter Family songs, and Pogo. He is a magic trunk too. One can never predict with accuracy what he will produce to astonish the beholders.

We first met in 1967 at an inner-city parish on the west side of Chicago where we worked in a summer program. We were worlds apart. Steve was still a student at Notre Dame, and I had just started teaching. We were even "romantically" teargassed the following summer at the Democratic National Convention but did not see each other again for several years.

Steve moved to Kansas City, worked in a campus minis-try program, and became more involved in opposition to the draft and the Vietnam War. Eventually, he spent five months in prison for refusing induction into the military.

Then in 1972 two important things happened to him: a camera and me. We were reintroduced by a chance phone call and his needing a place to stay in Chicago while visiting friends. He arrived with a 1938 Leica, a camera which his dad had originally bought in a pawnshop in Knoxville to take pictures of Steve when he was born. That was when I discovered the old trunk had a fake bottom which held a secret space I had never been in before.

Photography has become his way of exploring, poking around, and telling stories. For me it has meant getting used to being photographed at any time, any place. I remember brushing my teeth and hearing the shutter click for the first time. The everyday in our lives is dutifully recorded on hun-dreds of contact sheets. In fact, at times I feel Stephen is be-coming more like the creatures in Mammoth Cave which depend on the darkness for their existence. From his dark-room though have come images with faces I love to wander in. Different eyes for which I am thankful.

Kathleen Pelletier Moriarty